TO-MORROW IS A NEW DAY

TO-MORROW
IS A NEW DAY

By
JENNIE LEE

THE BOOK CLUB
121 Charing Cross Road
London, W.C.2

This edition 1941

PRINTED IN GREAT BRITAIN
BY WESTERN PRINTING SERVICES LTD., BRISTOL

For reasons that will be apparent to those who read it, this book is dedicated affectionately to my mother and father.

CHAPTER I

AN old tea caddy, complete with measuring spoon inside, stands on the corner of the mantelpiece in my mother's kitchen. It has stood there since 1900, the year when she was married. The measuring spoon was father's idea. It was more natural for mother to throw the tea leaves into the pot by the fistful.

Her lavish notions—it was the same with soup; half the town, father declared, could have been fed from her large black pot—were partly temperament, mainly habit.

For before her marriage mother was used to catering for a very large household. She did most of the cooking for her eleven brothers and sisters, and besides that, most of the kitchen work in a hotel and restaurant run by my maternal grandmother.

There was nothing fancy about Grandmother Greig's hotel. Scotch broth and Saturday night suppers of piping hot tripe and onions were its specialities. It gave good helpings at low prices.

The week-ends were its busiest times. It was then that young miners from the surrounding villages, eager for a bit of fun to break the monotony of the workaday week, made Cowdenbeath their centre.

A number of them would crowd into the restaurant, happy and carefree for an hour or two, making an unholy clatter with their laughter and banter.

My mother, the second eldest of Grandmother Greig's twelve children, was then a girl of nineteen. When people tell me that she was well liked by all the customers I can easily believe it. I can see her bustling around, quick moving but seldom flurried, making everyone feel comfortable, even a bit pampered. And the boundless goodwill she radiated around her kept everyone in a good humour even on the busiest of Saturday nights. That was more than forty years ago but she has not changed in the very least as anyone will tell you who has ever known her.

In 1899 one young miner began to appear in the restaurant suspiciously often. Grandmother Greig was not too pleased when she saw him come in. He was too ready to play practical jokes. And her tongue, which could bring most people to heel, had not the least effect on him. The more tartly she scolded, the more he seemed to enjoy himself.

By all accounts he was also a bit of a dandy. My mother still talks of the blue leather button boots he wore. She admired too his neat navy blue double-breasted suit. But there was one thing about him that rather disturbed her. No one could ever tell by looking at him whether it was the Sabbath or a weekday. He always wore the same neat navy blue double-breasted suit.

That was not as it should be. He ought to have had

2

an ordinary shifting suit for weekdays and something different for Sunday best. It made it not so bad when she discovered that he achieved his nattiness by having two suits exactly alike and wearing them alternately. But all the same a lurking feeling remained at the back of her mind that it was a bit disrespectful of the Sabbath not to make some sort of distinction.

Her interest in the good-looking young collier was practical and direct. She was hoping he would ask her to marry him. And so he did. In 1900 these two became man and wife and set up house together in the traditional Scotch but and ben.[1] They quickly assembled four children around them. I was the third of their children and know these early days only from hearsay.

They sound endlessly strenuous. At four o'clock in the morning the alarm-clock would ring. Before five the young husband had left for his work in the pit. A few hours later the young wife had set her house in order, washed and dressed her babies and was off with them to Grandmother Greig's hotel.

My father came to detest this hotel entanglement. He hated coming back from his work to a meal of odds and ends hurriedly assembled from the hotel kitchen. The day came when he laid down the law. His food had henceforth to be bought with his own wages and cooked under his own roof.

That was a blow for Grandmother Greig. She depended a good deal on the help of her married

[1] Two-roomed cottage.

3

daughter. But it never occurred to her to accept defeat. Her daughter was not coming to the hotel so often. Very well, the hotel must go to her daughter. So, piling all the hotel wash into the back of her old buggy, she drove off with it to her daughter's cottage. She had a very simple plan. Once at the cottage she dumped the soiled linen outside the door and let it be known that she would call again later in the week when it had all been nicely washed and dried. This scheme worked splendidly for a time. Then once again matters came to a head.

One day Grandmother Greig drove over as usual, the dirty linen piled up in the buggy behind her. But this time my father's mother was on the doorstep waiting for her. Grandmother Lee was also of a masterful disposition. The battle was pretty evenly drawn. In the end, however, Boadicea's buggy had to retire with the dirty linen still piled up inside it.

My mother, who then and always would do anything to keep the peace, remained indoors while all this was going on. She has told me since that she was "heavy footed" at the time. That is her reticent way of saying she was with child. Her second son was born soon afterwards. He died while still an infant.

All these things happened several years before I was born. My maternal grandmother had become bedfast and was rapidly dying when, as a very small child, I first remembered seeing her. She lay in a large canopied bed in a darkened room and had a way of putting her hand under the pillow, then fumbling for a long

4

time until she found her purse and slowly extracted a halfpenny which was given me for sweets.

Her illness meant that my mother had once again to do most of the work of the hotel. Ultimately my parents were persuaded to make the hotel their home. Then when my grandmother died they took over the business in their own name.

In these years Cowdenbeath was rapidly changing from a straggling village into a compact mining town. Old property was being pulled down. New buildings were going up everywhere.

Right in the centre of the town an arcade had appeared with shops on either side, a hall at the foot, and a hotel above the shops. The entrance to the hotel was half-way down the arcade.

Grandmother Greig's place of business had had to change with the changing town. Her old quarters were demolished and from 1902 onwards she rented the hotel above the grand new Arcade.

If modern advertising had been in fashion and the Arcade proprietors had been entirely immoral they might have given themselves a puff something like this:

"See Scotland where the past and present meet. The Arcade Hotel, High Street, Cowdenbeath, is on the Great North Road to the Highlands. Loch Leven with its good fishing and romantic memories of Mary Queen of Scots only five miles to the North. Dunfermline toune, the ancient capital of Scotland where

Bruce lies buried and where Malcolm Canmore and his gentle Margaret reigned, six miles to the west. Excellent cuisine and all modern conveniences."

It is very comical to think of the Arcade Hotel in these terms. Loch Leven and Dunfermline might just as well have been a thousand miles away. Especially in these days when there were few trains, no buses and the tramway line from Cowdenbeath to Dunfermline was a new-fangled novelty. Then, even more than now, the mining community was a world in itself. But no one could have been gaoled for a bogus advertisement of that kind. The location given would have been approximately right.

Actually the Arcade was a rickety structure of cheap red brick with a grey cement facing. Almost as soon as it was built it began to need heavy repairs and to look grimy and old. The most startling feature about it was the "pug" engine from the pit that went shunting to and fro at all hours of the day and night immediately below the hotel windows. The hotel was built where the level crossing cuts across the main street of the town. Strangers unaccustomed to the noise of the pug had small chance of an unbroken sleep.

But from my third to my eighth year (while it was my home) that second description gives no more idea of how the Arcade looked and felt to me than the first does.

From a child's angle it was a superb place. All kinds of exciting things were always happening. Particularly

6

in the hall at the foot of the Arcade. I could never be sure what new magic I would find there.

At that time touring companies were much in vogue. These were the great days of melodrama. East Lynne was drawing oceans of tears all over the country. The mining folks enjoyed a good cry as well as the next. They crowded into the Arcade Hall and by their patronage made it just worth while for companies travelling between Edinburgh and Perth to make Cowdenbeath an irregular place of call.

Between the visits of the theatre companies the hall was let to any organization that could pay the rent. It sheltered with equal readiness religious meetings, bird shows, wedding parties, funeral suppers, trade union lodge meetings, temperance lectures, the Clarion Scouts and the then active Social Democratic Federation. I patronized any of these gatherings that took my fancy. My mother was busy in the hotel upstairs. My father who had leased the hall was equally busy downstairs. No one had much time to pay attention to my comings and goings. I was able to run about pretty much as I pleased; and to collect a most dazzling range of acquaintances.

There was, for instance, my first love: a pleasant memory in spite of the grief he caused me. He was taller than any other man in the world and could carry me on his shoulder from room to room. He was not afraid to carry me through the kitchen to the back scullery where I was forbidden to go; and there he pilfered at my command small tin pastry shapes with

7

wriggles all round the edge that I wanted badly as playthings.

One day I was hanging out of the dining-room window looking on to the main street of the town waiting for him to come along. I saw him. He was seated on the top of a tram-car that was rumbling past. I waved, I shouted to him. But got no response. He did not even look my way. I collapsed in tears. The world had come to an end.

At the time that was all I knew. Since then I have learned that he was one-half of a variety turn called "The Long and the Short of It". He was the long half. They were travelling theatre people who were staying in the hotel. On the day in question my friend was nowhere to be found when the company assembled to prepare for the evening's performance. The short half went around frantically seeking for his partner. I was discovered damp and forlorn. From my story they decided that he had been dead drunk when he passed on the top of the tram-car and was riding blindly on towards the Dunfermline terminus. A rescue party was sent off post-haste to Dunfermline and there, indeed, they found him.

Another special friend of mine about this time was the Chinaman with the long pigtail. I refused to believe that the pigtail was real. Then one evening I was permitted to enter his room and watch his wife brush and braid it in readiness for the evening performance. As a final test I was allowed to pull as hard as I could. That settled it; I agreed it was real.

8

He was a splendid Chinaman, tall and benevolent and smiling. Someone told me that when Chinamen died they were buried face downwards so that their God could pull them straight up to Heaven by their pigtails. I cherished that bit of learning and have liked the Chinese ever since.

I am surprised how vividly I remember some things from these early days. There is no proper sequence or continuity about anything; just an assortment of odd bits and pieces. Tommy Torrance, trailing on to the stage of the Arcade Hall with his toy dog dragging behind him and singing "I'm happy for Life, I've lost my Wife and found a rare wee dug".[1] Sam Tamson playing his penny whistle and making us all laugh when he piped "I'm the saftest of the family, I'm the Simple Johnny Raw". Dr. Body terrifying us with his tricks. His adopted daughter, Dolly, who, in the deepest woman's voice that ever was, sang "Don't go down the mine, Daddy". (It was only later that we thought of parodies.) At that time we all cried.

Harry Lauder and Florrie Ford came to the Arcade along with the rest, but at the age of seven I could see nothing special about either of them. I preferred the ventriloquist with his doll. The doll was almost a young man in size. It could answer absolutely any question it was asked. Sometimes in the dressing-room behind the stage I had a special audience with it all to myself. Once I tried to pull it off its master's knee on

[1] Dog.

9

to my own, but its weight nearly knocked me over and it mumbled in an affronted tone of voice, "Don't do that".

I remember very little about my mother in those early hotel days. She was always busy. One day there was an extra stir in the kitchen. I suppose an unexpectedly large number of people had come into the dining-room and were clamouring for food. The bread supply ran out so I was bundled off to the baker's to bring back as much as I could carry. I bought delicious bread. It was still steaming hot straight from the bakehouse and had an odour that would have melted the heart of a stone. It got a bit squeezed on the way home but that could hardly be helped for the loaves were large square ones that doubled in like concertinas when I tried to make my arms go round them. I carried them home as best I could so was confused by the way I was raved at when I reached the kitchen door. My mother gave a cry of angry dismay. She was standing beside her bread-cutting machine at the large kitchen table. New bread, somehow, was no use to her. She wanted cutting bread she said.

I took her at her word and, summoning my baby brother, retired to a corner with the steaming loaves. Nobody wanted them, so they were ours, I reckoned, to do whatever we liked with. We put one each on our knees and hollowed out the soft warm hearts. That seemed a much nicer way of eating bread than having it handed you in monotonous slices.

The success of our little spree was short-lived.

10

Someone was shouting around the kitchen for the extra loaves. We were located in our corner and again somehow in disgrace. Apparently the loaves were wanted after all. But I had distinctly heard mother say that they were not what she wanted, that they were too new. It was all very perplexing and painful, not least the queer sensations in our insides. No one had ever told us that new bread eaten in hot chunks kept on swelling in your stomach until you felt like the whale with Jonah struggling about inside.

Another confused memory of the Arcade Hotel was the day when we thought our cat had been roasted in the oven. There was a sudden loud crack, then what looked like blood and entrails flowed out beneath the oven door. Mother flew forward, opened the door, and oh! what a relief! It was only Jam-jars up to his tricks again. Jam-jars was the name everyone gave to one of the hotel boarders who refused to eat any food cooked in the ordinary way. He prepared his own meals, cooking everything in jam-jars. This day his jar had burst. I have not the slightest recollection of what Jam-jars looked like, but I remember very plainly our large, slow-moving black cat and the agony that seized us when the bursting of the jam-jar made us think we had sent it to an awful death.

There was little time or place for domestic pets in that busy hotel household. Rats were the animals I saw and heard most about. A trap used to be set for them under the sink in the back kitchen. They were both terrible and irresistible. When I knew there were dead ones lying on the scullery floor, I wanted to run to the other end of the building—and I knew I would have to creep near enough to see their ugly faces and glassy, bulging eyes.

I probably remember the rats so well because of a fight I once saw between my father and a live one. It was upstairs on the bedroom floor in a small turret box-room. There was no furniture in the room. My father was standing in the middle of the floor with a long stick in his hand. The Devil incarnate in the body of an enormous rat was glaring at him with all Hell in its eyes. I had heard a scuffle and looked into the room in aimless curiosity. I was not prepared for this terrible sight. Father lifted the stick. The rat, cornered by now, crouched and glared, ready to spring at his throat. Then it leapt!—leapt right over his shoulder and out of the one small window quite high up in the room. When anyone talks of a cornered rat the picture that lives in me is quite definite and clear. I see the old Arcade, the small turret room, the window, my father, and that leaping grey embodiment of evil and of the disease that lay in the stinking burn at the back of the hotel. The rats, I was told, came from the burn. I hated and feared both.

There was quite a lot that was gloomy and threatening in that grey, ramshackle building. The smoking-room, for instance, had only one window and that looked out on a blank wall. It let in almost no light. The gas had to be lit even during the day. But it was important to go into the smoking-room sometimes for there was a huge dark side-board there and in a glass case on the top of the sideboard three most wonderful dolls, as large as life. No one was allowed to play with the dolls or even to touch them. They belonged to my grandmother who had bought them at a sale and had given them (nominally) to her youngest daughters. But that was long ago and these daughters were now too old for dolls, so it seemed hard that they should stand there out of reach of all the grandchildren who were itching to get at them. It was only after my grandmother died that the case was opened and the dolls distributed. I got one of them. But after it ceased to be untouchable it must have impressed me much less. I can remember no more about it.

People used to say that if ever fire broke out in the Arcade it would be a death-trap. There was no fire-escape. There was not even a back stair. This infuriated my mother. It meant that all the refuse had to be carried out of the main entrance. Also the roof was continually leaking. So any little profit she had for all her hard work was eaten up in repapering the bed-rooms, and other essential repairs.

But none of these worries weighed on my six or seven years. In spite of damp and rats and gloomy corridors and the bad smell from the burn, the odds and ends I remember from that time have a pleasant colouring. It was my parents who had all the worries; my mother in particular, who had to be up at dawn and rubbing and scrubbing and cooking and serving without rest for a single hour during the whole long day. She always worked much harder than anyone she engaged to help her. Her fatal defect was that she was much quicker and better at doing things herself than at ordering anyone else to do them for her. She almost killed herself with the work, but the only one who made any profit out of the place was the landlord.

The Arcade belonged to one of Grandmother Greig's many brothers. He paid us a visit once a year to fish in Loch Leven and collect his rent. Rather to our consternation, he was in the habit of kissing us all when he arrived and departed, an alien custom he must have picked up among the English. Scotch folks are not given to greeting their relatives so demonstratively.

In other ways this uncle was unlike any other member of his family. Starting life, quite literally, as a bare-footed boy peddling shoe-laces from door to door, he accumulated quite a comfortable fortune. His single-minded interest in money-making gave him an advantage over most people. Over Grandfather Greig, for instance, who loved his fiddle and loved his dram but had not the least scrap of business capacity. It was probably just as well therefore that he should have been induced to sign over his share in some property my great-grandmother then possessed for five shillings, the price of a drink or two.

Grandfather Greig spent the last years of his life roving about the countryside, usually sleeping in model lodging-houses. His children tried again and

14

again to salvage him. But he had no liking for their settled, respectable lives. That they could never understand.

My mother who has an invincible gift for making excuses for everybody, makes them for him with more than her usual warmheartedness. He was nobody's enemy but his own, she will say. He had no bad in him. He would not have hurt a fly. And, clinching every other argument, at sixty she still tenderly recalls how, when they were all young children at home together, Grandfather Greig would make them happy by playing his fiddle to them. Sometimes, for their very special delight he would make his fiddle say "Ma-ma, Pa-pa".

Before I was quite eight years old my parents moved out of the hotel into a small private house. There was no inducement for them to remain in the business. It had become quite clear that the uncle proprietor had no intention of modernizing the place. Also, although my mother was in her familiar environment, my father must have been about the strangest business "gent" it is possible to imagine. He was not then, or at any time, a gloomy spoil-sport. But he had strong social and political convictions which he clung to with dogged persistence. For one thing, he insisted on the business remaining a "Temperance" Hotel. That was considered a great hardship by jaded commercial travellers and thirsty theatrical people. And, on top of that, to be met by an eager landlord anxious to sell them a copy of "Merrie England" or "Britain for the British"

15

was more than ordinary mortals could be expected to stand.

It is customary now to decorate nursery schools, and the infants' department in ordinary schools, with gaily coloured toys and pictures. There was little or none of that when I went to school. That was in the years just before the war. School was a drab, grey routine of unexciting tasks. But the stern old gods that frown down from our northern skies were cheated in my case. The Arcade was my real nursery school. Its actors and actresses, rats and ventriloquist's doll, its toy shop and Chinaman with a real pigtail, form in my memory a frieze of as grotesque and brightly coloured pictures as any child's artists could devise.

If we had gone on living there it would no doubt have looked different as I learned to see my surroundings with older eyes. But from eight years onwards, there was no more hotel life. Instead there was the usual routine of a small working-class household.

The hotel world faded entirely out of the picture. I do not remember even recalling it. We were caught up and completely absorbed in my father's life, which was entirely that of the mining community to which he again unequivocally belonged.

This incursion into hotel-keeping, so far as my father was concerned, was purely accidental. After an absence of a few years he went back to the pits where he had begun to work when he was twelve years old, where his brothers and his friends were working and where his father had worked for twenty-nine years. Grand-

16

father Lee had, by that time, ceased working underground but he would have been very indignant if
anyone had said he was no longer a miner.

His workmates had elected him a full-time official of
the Fife Miners' Union.

CHAPTER II

THE great thing about moving into a four-roomed private house was the discovery that we now had a garden. There was none at the hotel; only a large, dreary piece of waste land with the stinking burn at the foot of it.

When I first saw our strip of garden it was glorified by a patch of white blossom. I thought it would be a fine thing to pluck all this loveliness and carry it off to school. Just as I had finished my good-tempered mother, so seldom angry, came rushing out, scolding vehemently. It seemed that I had ravaged the strawberry bed, that every flower would later have been a large red berry, but that now, because of what I had done, we would have no strawberries that year. I liked flowers; but I liked strawberries too. It was a sad beginning.

Our home was now one of a monotonous row of houses in a typical working-class side street. There is no subtlety about the way such houses are designed. A narrow lobby ran through the centre of the house with two doors on either side. The two front rooms overlooking the street—there was no front garden—were used as bedrooms. One of the back rooms was the

18

kitchen-living-room, the other a bedroom and sitting-room combined. The lavatory was always a source of annoyance to my mother. It was at the inside end of the lobby. If the door was left open it looked out directly on to the street. She did her best with it by draping a curtain over the entrance.

A still bigger nuisance was that once again we had no back door. All ashes and refuse had to be carried out on to the front pavement, then down a long draughty close to the back garden. The coal cellar and washhouse were also at the back of the house. This was doubly hard on mother for her eyes troubled her. Each time she went hurrying through the draughty close, the cold biting winds kept them reddened and sore. But for all that, by the time we rushed home from school in the middle of the afternoon, our kitchen was a very pleasant place to run into. There was sure to be a bright fire burning in the open grate, a white cloth spread on the table promising that tea would soon be ready, and, if the kettle was not already singing, we thought we had a grievance. Sometimes there was also the pleasant odour of scones and pancakes freshly baked for tea.

The only time we were really uncomfortable at home was Saturday forenoons. There was no school on Saturday. Mother did her extra week-end cleaning then and we were expected to lend a hand. I was not a great success. It would be too much to say that I disliked housework. I was just negative about it. So negative that I usually forgot what I was about and settled down on top of the large chest-of-drawers with the glass-doored bookcase on top. That was where our best and biggest books were kept. Right in front of me would be *The Arabian Nights*, *Das Kapital*, *The Family Physician*, *Ingersol's Lectures and Essays*, *The Count of Monte Cristo*, *Science History of the Universe*, *The Brass Check*, *White Fang*, *The Three Musketeers*. Before I quite realized what was happening I was the Count of Monte Cristo tapping away desperately in an effort to establish communication with the prisoner in the next cell. Or I was Liza fleeing from slavery across the broken ice and carrying a child in my arms. Or Burning Daylight swaggering into town, the toughest and whitest man in all the North.

Once having started a book I hated having to lay it down before I had read right through to the very end. But, on Saturday forenoons, I was handicapped by a most inconvenient conscience. This kept telling me, to my infinite irritation, "There's work to do, work to do, work to do". If my mother had been in any sense a martinet I rather think I would have fought back at her and enjoyed it. But, supposing you should want to defy mother, there was no way of knowing where to begin. She had not the slightest idea of how to be exacting or stern. I knew that if I did not speedily hop down from the top of the drawers and rub and scrub and dust for dear life to make up for time lost, she would simply do the whole of the week-end cleaning herself without even being sulky about it.

Sometimes I came near to breaking her temper (a

considerable achievement) in the early part of Saturday afternoon. It was then that the special week-end shopping had to be done. Mother always declared that she preferred doing this herself. But there was so much for her to do at home that most Saturdays she had to depend on me.

I would be sent off to go through one department after another of our local Co-operative, and bring home the week's supplies. Always I was told to be careful with the eggs. Always I told myself that this time there would be no accident. But at least one (sometimes more) had a miserable habit of getting itself broken. I never quite knew how it happened. I was too absent-minded, mother would storm. I must stop day-dreaming and remember what I was about. It astounded me that there should be so many mishaps, particularly as I had my own illegitimate reason for trying to remember not to swing the basket with the eggs in it. For, when shouting across the store grocery counter "a pound of ham (must be lean), a packet of matches, a tin of creamola, half a pound of the best Ceylon tea, a packet of self-raising flour, two pounds of sugar", what harm was there in adding—"and two-penny worth of candy mixtures". No harm that I could ever see, especially as there were large boxes of sweets propped up on the counter that kept staring at me all the time I was waiting to be served. But mother's view about that unauthorized twopence worth was different. The only hope of getting off with it was for the rest of the groceries to be in ship-shape order. If the eggs were broken, then you could be sure there would be a double fuss; one for the eggs, and one for the mixtures.

Truth to tell, her scoldings were never very terrible. But if sorely tried she would add—"and if you do that again I'll tell your father". That was disturbing. There was always the possibility that one time she actually would. And what then? Our father never bullied and never used baby talk. He had a way of treating us as if we were responsible grown-ups. That was very flattering. We liked it. But the other side of the account was that we were anxious not to fall into his "black books". A talking to from him occurred only once or twice in a lifetime. It was a serious affair not to be met with lighthearted banter in the way we treated our mother's scoldings.

If Saturday forenoon was stormy and strenuous, the rest of the week-end made up for it. By teatime at the latest, we could settle down to real luxury. Everything at home, the fire and the firearms, and the brass trays and candlesticks on the mantelpiece above the fire, dazzling to look at. Not that we bothered about that sort of thing. We had more important business on hand. For it was then the great moment came when we were given our Saturday pennies and could dash off to buy our weekly quota of one penny fairy-tale and two comic-cuts. I chose the fairy-tale, my brother the comics. We each devoured our own, then eagerly swopped.

In a southern country, life, I imagine, must turn

outwards a great deal towards the sun. In this dreary, industrial north our life turned inwards instead. There was not much to attract us out of doors. For months in the year a grey drizzle fell dejectedly from an uninviting sky. There was seldom even good, clean snow; just dirty sludge, part snow, part rain, part coal-dust. Even in the summer evenings we usually clustered around the fire. For in Scotland the summers are short and precarious; winter weather takes up most of the year.

During all my schooldays our kitchen fireside was the centre of the world. We were very contented when we were allowed to sprawl on the rug in front of the fire with our story-books spread out around us. "Tell me a story," my small brother would demand. That was easy. We had only to look into the flames and very soon giants and hobgoblins and weird animals paraded in front of us. We had to be on the alert to see them for they stayed only a minute fraction of time then vanished again down the sun-coloured caverns behind the rocks of coals. We were fire-worshippers, and never grew tired of it.

Sometimes at home in the evening it was very quiet outside with only one sound breaking the stillness; the beat of the ventilation-fan at the neighbouring pit. That regular beat, beat, beat, invaded our fireside. It got tangled up with the giants and ogres we were reading about. We invented stories in which the pit was a monster and the rhythmic noise we heard, the beating of its heart. This monster dragged

23

all kinds of victims to their doom. It imprisoned them in its gaunt dungeon. Then brave knights would ride to the rescue. At first every knight met with danger and defeat. The faint-hearted turned back. Even the bravest were disheartened sometimes. But, in the end, we always allowed them to set the captives free.

One day we found our father reading a book called the *Octopus*. He explained, when we pestered him, what "octopus" meant. We promptly decided that the pit was an octopus. It had arms stretching in all directions. It sucked in everything around it.

In these days our father was the all-wise and infallible one. He taught us our sums a year ahead of school schedule. Without ever preaching at us, he taught us a great deal more besides. His critical socialist outlook influenced our attitude to everything around us. We knew that beyond our sheltered fireside there were evil spirits abroad. And we knew that he was one of the good knights and true who would one day slay all the dragons and set poor people free.

This "we" I keep talking about was not a large company. I ought to have had three brothers, but two died before I was old enough to remember much about them. The third was two and a half years younger than I was. We were inseparable. He was a gentle and loving child. Our mother had a habit of humming and singing out of tune as she went about her work. One day, for some reason, she was worried and low-spirited. He always noticed that sort of thing. Tugging at her skirt, he tried to find out what was the matter. To

24

satisfy him she had to start humming and making cheerful faces. He was just as foolish about animals. There was almost always a stray dog or cat sheltering in our back garden. The mangiest-looking creatures, they usually were. But you could be sure he would wait on them as if they were visiting Royalty.

Our mother strictly forbade us to bring dogs and cats into the house. Dogs, she said, brought dirt and smells with them. Cats were forbidden because of our canary. That bird was the drabbest, most rickety-looking little proletarian it was possible to behold. It was brought from the pit one day in a minute, coal-blackened prison of a cage. I remember my father plomping it down beside the kitchen sink and saying "Poor devil, it deserves to live". Greatly marvelling, we listened to its story. Six times it had been sent into working places in the pit where the air was bad. Each time, by dropping off its perch, overcome by gas-fumes, it gave warning to the men that it was time for them to move out. The seventh time, when our father was pumping oxygen into it to revive it, he decided that it was time for the little collier bird to go into honourable retirement. At the end of the shift he brought it to the surface with him and home. That same evening, before the shops closed, we went out together and bought it as large and fine a cage as our small funds would run to. We were always proud when our friends remarked on how gaily it sang. And, prejudice apart, it really did sing remarkably well.

Although indoor pets were banned, one day my

brother was allowed to invest his whole fortune—he had four shillings and sevenpence in his money-box—in a rabbit hutch and a small rabbit. He was in heaven. But as the days passed strange things began to happen. His pet's appetite was enormous. We trespassed over every garden in the neighbourhood searching for dandelion leaves for it. We made it immense helpings of a mixture of oatmeal and old tea-leaves that rabbits were supposed to like. It never seemed to stop eating. And the strong stench from its hutch that we were in honour bound to keep clean, was distressing. Worst of all, when we brought it out beside us on the green, hoping to stroke it and watch it scamper gently about our feet, it raced off at lightning speed and jumped over every garden wall and fence within sight. We had to chase after it as best we could. A growing suspicion began to haunt us. At last it would no longer be denied. Our rabbit was a whacking big hare. In spite of that, my brother clung to it tenaciously and would never admit that it had a single fault.

Some time before this he had his fifth birthday. It was time for him to go to school. And it was my job to take him there. That term nearly all my class seemed to be dragging younger brothers and sisters to their first days of schooling. Some yelled, others walked along quite trustingly. The great thing was to see whose charge would be at the head of the line when the infant class assembled in the playground ready to march into school after the forenoon interval. We older ones, each clutching a hapless infant of five would eye one another suspiciously then fight and push for position. It took careful generalship for we were not supposed to be in the infants' playground. As soon as the teachers appeared in sight we had to fly off to our own part of the grounds. In those school bouts I usually won. I was not fair and gentle like my brother. I was dark and stubborn.

After having started the child at school, my next concern was to make sure that he would one day go to heaven. At nine years old I was devoutly religious in a very concrete and primitive way. Hell was Hell and I saw it vividly exactly as it was described to me— as a great big burning fire. Scotland, especially the Scotland of the older generation, is prone to take its religion gloomily. We talked of God-fearing men— very seldom of God-loving ones. The punishments lying in wait for the sinner loomed much larger on our youthful horizon than any pleasure that might be the reward of virtue. Hell always seemed a much more tangible and likely proposition than any conceptions we had of Heaven. My anxiety over theological matters was deepened by the fact that my parents were not church-goers. I secretly envied one of my little play-mates whose father could be seen every Sunday walking solemnly to church wearing a tall silk hat, a tail-coat and gloves. He was a deacon. I had no idea what that meant but I felt that somehow we lost caste by having a father who had a tail-coat and a tall hat hanging at the back of the wardrobe but who would not wear them even to funerals.

27

Those social problems were important; but small enough in comparison with my concern as to what would become of us all in the next world, especially my brother. At all costs I was anxious that he should be saved. I did what I could by seeing that he never forgot to say his prayers both night and morning.

I remember one night, after we were both tucked up in bed, waking with a start for prayers had been forgotten. I can distinctly recall kicking him out of bed, tearful and protesting and not allowing him back again until he had prayed long and thoroughly. His tears had no effect on me for I saw the Hell flames leaping in the background. It was all for his own good. I was resolved that there should be no mishap where he was concerned. For myself, I mumbled all the words of the prayer but remained inside the blankets, knowing that was not so efficacious as kneeling on the cold floor but hoping it would do.

Apparently I succeeded in instilling into him a wholesome fear of the Almighty, assisted, about this time, by a terrible accident. One of the few things that were strictly forbidden in our household was bathing in the Netherton Burn. The Netherton was a small winding stream more than a mile from home. We were told it was dirty and dangerous. It looked shallow and clean enough, and on a really warm day could be quite inviting. One day my brother ran off with a group of other boys and succumbed to temptation. Against strictest orders he went dookin' in the burn. I knew nothing of this until after I had been in bed some time and all the lights were out. A shivering bundle of misery woke me by creeping into my bed. He was sobbing pitifully. God had punished him. One of his boots had been lost in the burn. Worse than that, it was a new boot worn that day for the first time. He had searched for it desperately as long as the light lasted, then slunk home, leaving the odd boot behind the outside door and hurrying straight to bed so as not to be found out.

I don't know how such a thing would seem to a child in a well-to-do household. For us it was the end of the world. Much more than disobedience was involved. There was the cash side as well. Boots cost a lot of money. I could hear what mother would say: "Your father has been down the pit all day knocking his soul-case out to get you boots and this is what you do. Two days' work thrown into the burn". That was how we reckoned money. It was a sombre form of reckoning. Certain things cost half a shift. Others a whole shift. Some even more than that. Boots were one of the big items that had to be "saved" for. They had to be treated with respect. And here was a brand-new boot—it might as well have been both—lying at the bottom of the burn.

I comforted the sinner as best I could, telling him I would make it all right with his father and mother, that God had already punished him enough. I was lying valiantly. I could hardly see how any mercy could be hoped for. They were very good boots. The best quality the Co-op stocked. It was terrifying to think of it.

When morning came I did my diplomatic best. But there was no way of putting it that did not come at last to the hideous, inescapable truth—one of the new boots was buried in the burn.

Mother gave a sharp moan. I could see from her face that it was as bad as I had feared. Half begging, half bullying, I extorted the promise that father was to know nothing about it. We arranged that, immediately school was over, we would both go with her and have another search for the boot. We went, but it was useless. All our rummaging and plunging failed to bring up anything except old tin cans and a drowned cat.

That same year, or perhaps a year later, another boot incident darkened the world. It was Christmas Eve. We had written our letters to Santa Claus, hung up our stockings, and gone confidently to bed. I woke in the middle of the night and peered out to see what could be seen. There, clear as could be, was my stocking with a bulge in the middle of it and a new box lying beside the fireplace. I got up at once and found in the stocking one miserable and lonely orange. In the box there was a new pair of brown long-legged boots. Mad with resentment I strutted back to bed and wept bitter, scalding tears of anger. This was an outrage. Boots indeed. Everyone had to have boots, Christmas or no Christmas. To palm off boots as a Santa Claus gift was contemptible. Santa Claus was

supposed to bring things you wanted, not just things
you had to have anyway. To bring boots of all things
was mockery and theft. It was an unjust world. A
harsh malignant world. I wanted to sleep and not wake
up again unless perhaps to slay people. On Christmas
morning I woke late, dazed and stupefied. It was
difficult piecing things together. What had happened
during the night? What was happening now? For
there, clustered all around the fireplace were stacks of
boxes overflowing with toys and story-books. Gradually
I saw what must have happened. I had frightened off
my parents when they were just beginning to lay out
our gifts. Now it was morning and everything was as
it should be, and yet not quite everything. That
Christmas day was less carefree than others I remembered. The bitter tears at dawn had left their mark.
They made a difference when I walked off to school
with the pick of my presents under my arm. I was not
so jaunty and noisily boastful as I had sometimes been
on these occasions. With a *Chatterbox* under one arm
and a double-jointed doll under the other, I ran full
tilt into a meek little girl who always hovered about the
foot of the class. We compared notes. Once I had gone
through my list of presents, not leaving out even the
new brown long-legged boots, I asked for hers. Santa
Claus had brought her an orange and a penny and a
miserable squirt of a cotton handkerchief with rabbits
in the corner. I was appalled. Her home was one of the
poorest in the town. There was a large family of
young ones. Their clothes were always shabby and

31

worn. They never seemed to have any toys of their own. I looked at her warily. Had she been raving and storming earlier in the morning as I would have done? There were no signs of rage or bitterness or envy. She fingered my new doll in a quiet, gentle way. I could not even be quite sure she would have liked to have had one like it. I was afraid to ask her in case she said yes or cried. I don't think she would have shown much sign of feeling even if I had inquired. She was one of the meek who, I had heard somewhere, were to inherit the earth. She did not look like an heiress.

This encounter worried me. There were many others at school who had received little or nothing for Christmas. I was one of the plutocrats. The only others who had more imposing loot than myself were the children of business people whom we thought very rich. It worked out like a lesson in arithmetic. The richer you were the more you got. If you had nothing at all, you got nothing. I knew Santa Claus was partly one's parents but, in addition to that, there was a mystical glow about the season of Christmas and the hint that some other spirit was abroad. I developed a mordantly critical mood towards this other spirit, this spirit of Christmas. So Santa Claus was what the men in the pits would call a belly-crawler. The old gentleman with the red gown and white beard and benevolent air liked to keep in with the gaffer. He toadied to those who already had most and left out in the cold those who hung up their stockings with the biggest emptinesses needing to be filled. He brought me, who

32

already had a share in one penny fairy-tale and two comic-cuts every Saturday afternoon, several fat volumes of stories and other things as well. He brought this pale, inoffensive little schoolmate, who had no story-books, no best quality Co-op boots, no doll, no anything, a tawdry handkerchief, a penny and an orange. There was something wrong somewhere. I felt I must have a consultation with my father, who knew everything and was always just. I can still remember fragments of that particular talk. Capitalism, I learned, had "neither a body to kick nor a soul to save. There would have to be a Revolution". I felt blown-up with all this information, but not much wiser.

There was a great variation in the home-life of the children I grew up beside. Some, like myself, had comfortable homes, never had to go hungry, and, in addition to weekday clothes, had a special set of everything to be worn only on the Sabbath. Others lived in dismal, smelly, overcrowded quarters, never saw a freshly-starched white tablecloth, had poor food with little nourishment value, and sometimes in winter time came to school with no soles to their boots or wearing cheap canvas shoes that drew water like sponges and gave them chilblains.

Ours was a mining community and we were almost all miners' children. But, if there were six or eight in the family and all too young to be earning anything, it made an unbelievable difference to the kind of shelter and food that the family could afford. Even where there was a small family, it needed steady work,

D

careful spending and some extra money coming in from somewhere before there could be any real comfort.

From a miner's wage there was little over for such flippances as, for instance, filling Christmas stockings. My brother and myself got more than most. We ran a regular racket at Christmas-time. Weeks, sometimes months, before, we badgered a young jeweller who lodged with us, to write our letter to Santa Claus. At that time he was a lonely bachelor and so an easy prey. We reckoned that if he wrote the Christmas letter he would not be able to make a mistake about what we wanted; and we were unblushing in our demands. He never failed us. He drew out the list of requests in the order of their urgency, blew the letter up the chimney and we found it politic to pretend we believed in the old man in the reindeer-sledge years after we had discovered the truth. I doubt if he was seriously taken in by our ruses, but he played up—and paid up— handsomely all the same.

CHAPTER III

WHEN I was nine years old I must have known every word of *Robinson Crusoe* off by heart. I had a very special reason for this. Our father had told us that Lower Largo was the birthplace of Robinson Crusoe. Our mother had booked a room in Upper Largo for the miners' holiday week. The whole town knew of these goings on. We babbled for months beforehand of this coming holiday by the sea.

Then came the deadly warning. We were cautioned not to build our hopes too high. There were rumours of a strike that was to be the biggest ever known in the history of mining. Every pit in the whole of Great Britain was to be brought to a standstill. If there was a strike, there could be no holiday. For days longer than years we hung around in an agony of suspense. As children it seemed a matter of life and death to us that no strike should take place just at that time. We pleaded with our parents, trying to make them understand that the most important thing in the world was that we should go to Robinson Crusoe's birthplace. We badgered all we dared. When our tongues were silenced our eyes went on campaigning.

Eventually the family conference was held where

our fate had to be decided. Our mother looked inquiringly towards father. It was his place to give a lead. Two disconsolate children were hanging on his every word. He went on smoking his pipe in a slow, tantalizing way he sometimes has then began very slowly and deliberately: "As likely—as not—there will be—a strike. But nothing—is definite yet.—We might—as well risk it."

Oh, the relief! That was all we wanted to know. We could run off now and prepare for our ascension straight into heaven.

I can always return to Largo Bay with a special feeling of intimacy and pleasure. Its old grey harbour is quite lovely. It is peaceful in the uplands behind the sea.

But that is not the Largo we knew as children. That Largo was a place of pure magic. The fishermen down by the harbour in their great blue jerseys filled us with bashful hero worship. Sometimes they let us sit in their boats. Once or twice we were taken a little way out to sea.

Then there were the Pierrots. Such Pierrots. We never willingly missed a performance. We liked the funny songs and we liked the sentimental ones. We liked everything. One day the favourite comedian caught sight of our parents. Without stopping his songs and patter, he lifted his hat and called "How are you, Mr. Lee?" A minute later in the midst of his fooling he sang out again, "And how's our Mrs. Lee? I am coming round to see". No one in the audience except ourselves knew that these words had any meaning. But we knew.

36

My brother and I nudged each other with pride and pleasure. Later, jingling the collection bag, he made his way to our part of the crowd. He really was a special friend of ours. He had stayed in the Arcade Hotel years before we were born.

On the second day of our holiday we got the news from somewhere that quite definitely there would be no strike. A settlement had been reached. That same day, trailing down to the beach together, my father and I stopped to buy a newspaper. He read it when we reached the shore, then stared gravely out to sea. So gravely that I knew something was seriously wrong. I was filled with dark misgivings. Perhaps there was going to be a strike after all. Perhaps we would have to return home that very day. Even if we could stay our whole week, perhaps there would be no pennies for ice-cream and everyone would be looking gloomy. I asked what was wrong. Would there be a strike? No, there would be no strike but the Germans—the German Fleet. Now I could breathe again. There was to be no strike. We could finish our holiday in peace. That was July 1914.

When the war began we collected all the broken dolls we could lay hands on and played at hospitals. Those with limbs missing were in special demand. And, of course, it was not possible for us to attend to our wounded until we had uniforms and white head-dresses like other nurses. When our mothers were not looking we confiscated old white towels and handkerchiefs and improvised magnificently.

We had lots of fine war games. But as the weeks passed I began to feel disquieted. My parents were not cheering with the rest of the crowd. They were opposed to the war. This was awkward. It was worse than that, it was frightening. I dared not confess it, but secretly I felt ashamed. Children are sticklers for convention. They hate their family to seem in any way "queer". Yet here we were meeting each Sunday evening in the open-air miles outside the town because the local authorities and someone called D.O.R.A.[1] refused to give us permission to hold meetings in the usual places like ordinary people. Then one Sunday evening I became happy and proud and spiritually at one with my family. It was one of those rare Sundays in Scotland when it is gloriously warm even in the evening. I had walked out to the Netherton Burn, where our meetings were usually held, along with my parents and two visiting I.L.P. propagandists. They were to speak to us about the war. I don't remember a word of what they said but I recall very vividly a conversation I was holding with myself while the meeting was in progress. That week in school our history lesson had dealt with the persecution of the old Covenanters and their secret meetings on lonely hillsides. True, we were meeting at the side of a busy main road and beckoning to all who passed to come and listen. Nor had any of our members been put on the rack or tortured with thumb-screws. But the parallel was near enough. Were we not a persecuted minority? Were not some of our members

[1] "Defence of the Realm Act".

in prison? Were we not forced to meet in the open country miles outside the town? Were not terrible things done to some of our men while they were in gaol? I had just overheard some talk about a conscientious objector who refused to wear khaki so was stripped naked and left like that. When he still refused to wear soldier's uniform, he was laid on a table and scrubbed from head to foot with a wire-brush until his flesh was torn and bleeding. That decided it. We were the modern Covenanters, we were fighting for conscience' sake. There were only a few of us, but it was we, not the multitude who were right. That conclusion made things much easier. Nothing could now make me feel ashamed. Indeed, I was now ready to go forth to battle and to slaughter everyone who stood in our way.

During the war years, Duncan Beaton, a local miner, Mrs. Watson, wife of the present Member for Dunfermline Burghs, and Mr. Garvie, the blind bookseller, conducted a flourishing socialist Sunday School. I learned to recite with great gusto a poem called the "Image of God". It went something like this:

> *I slaughtered a man, a brother,*
> *In the wild, wild fight at Mons,*
> *I see yet his eyes of terror,*
> *Hear yet his cries and groans.*

Every one of us without exception was made word-perfect in the ten socialist precepts. I thought the one about war very reasonable. "Do not think that those who love their own country need hate or despise other nations or wish for war, which is a remnant of barbarism."

Mrs. Henderson, a miner's wife with a strong, sweet voice, attended every Sunday forenoon to help us with the singing. We learned to sing after her:

> *O beautiful my country,*
> *Be it thy nobler care;*
> *Than all thy wealth of commerce,*
> *Thy harvests waving fair.*
> *Be it thy pride to lift up*
> *The manhood of the poor,*
> *Be thou to the oppressed*
> *Fair freedom's open door.*

After that we all joined in the chorus:

> *We are children, but some day,*
> *We'll be big and strong and say,*
> *None shall slave and none shall slay,*
> *Comrades all together.*

We shall up and march away, march away, march away,
We shall up and march away, marching all together.

Another important part of my wartime training was a cartoon I picked up among my father's papers. It showed a monkey sitting in the tree-tops and looking quizzically down on a vast plain where men were fighting, maiming and killing one another. The caption underneath read "Thank God civilization missed me". I thought that very fine. I was now a politician and one with very definite views.

When the war had been on for some time and food rationing was at its strictest, my brother became ill. He needed more nourishment than the ration-cards allowed. My mother went to the Town House and applied for a permit for extra rations of meat and eggs. She was told that she must first get a doctor's certificate. The doctor called the following day. After a long examination he looked grave and said there was a small spot on one of the child's lungs. That way of putting it did not help. I knew that meant an early stage of consumption. The doctor then advised sending him to a sanatorium. I felt sick and panicky.

For the next three months the war was not important. I learned no more poetry and didn't care whether we were Covenanters or not. All that mattered was our weekly visits to a small boy lying in the bed fifth from the door in the children's ward of Thornton Sanatorium. He was made to wear a grey flannel nightshirt. I was angry and sad every time I saw that awful garment. It made me think of gaols and poor-houses. Why couldn't he wear his own clothes? I petitioned the nurses about it. They answered me civilly but firmly. It was a hospital regulation. And hospitals will be hospitals—when poor people are the inmates.

Each Saturday I walked through the fields to the sanatorium. The bus went only part of the way. When the snow was on the ground it was a bleak, tiring journey. I discovered that the best way of carrying parcels was in a net bag slung over my shoulder. I was too proud to arrive carrying it that way so, when the last corner was in sight, I swung it down and hung it nonchalantly over one arm. Once round the corner I could see the sanatorium and the glass door at the end of the ward. It was usually open. With any luck I could tip-toe right to the bedside without asking anyone's permission. And, knowing how I hated cold, my brother would thrust my hands and head beneath the blankets on his bed, and would have to be satisfied that I had thawed before he would even look at his parcels. To our great joy, three months later he was home again looking comically round and red and greatly improved in health. I could now go on with the war.

Shortly after this the war became almost real. My mother's youngest brother was killed in action. We all sat down together and wept, then, about a week later, the socks that had been knitted for him were sent to another uncle who was in the trenches. It became still more real when my closest friend at school arrived with red swollen eyes and wearing a black dress. Her father had been killed in action. All of us in the class tried in clumsy little ways to show our sympathy. I thrust before her all my answers in the arithmetic tests, although in the ordinary course of things it was arithmetic I depended on to pull me above her in our battles for first place in class.

But we were young and soon forgot those things.

The meetings held by the I.L.P. to explain the causes of the war and how to end it made a much more lasting impression on me than anything else I remember from those years.

One evening, greatly daring, it was decided to attempt an anti-war meeting some miles from home, practically at the gates of a military camp. David Kirkwood was the speaker. My father was in the chair. Before the meeting could begin a great hulking brute of a fellow caught my father in the ribs and threw him right over the heads of the crowd. Kirkwood immediately jumped on the chair that served as a platform and, brandishing a stout stick in the air, roared out: "If there is a better man than me here, let him come and take this platform."

Both soldiers and civilians in the audience enjoyed that kind of pacifism. Order was soon restored. A rough house of that kind seldom occurred when the audience was made up exclusively of miners. Experience varied in different coalfields. Here I am recording simply moods and circumstances as I recall them in our corner of Fife. And I am referring to public meetings, not to miners' lodge meetings.

Within the union, Grandfather Lee, then Disputes Agent for the Fife Miners' Union, was almost the only official who stood out against the war. I have heard since how the other officials, led by the late Mr. W. Adamson, who were all violently pro-war, did everything in their power to make life Hell for him.

When the war began I was not yet ten years of age and when it ended I was barely fourteen, so its tragedies and controversies sat lightly upon me. But it made our home a very busy place. The few active local socialists who were campaigning against the war were constantly coming in and out for odd meals and discussion.

The week-ends were crammed with events. Very often we had a visiting I.L.P. propagandist staying with us. Usually he came from Glasgow, occasionally from London, and sometimes he was a young fellow on the run from place to place wanted by the police for his anti-war activities.

Those Saturdays when the speaker's train was due to arrive before father could be home from work, washed and changed, it was my job to go to the station. I liked that. It was always a tense moment waiting for the train to draw into the platform. If it was someone who had been with us before, then he was a friend and sure of his welcome. If it was a stranger arriving for the first time, it was a different, but equally pleasant kind of excitement. It was like putting your hand into a lottery bag and drawing out a ticket. You never knew what was going to turn up. Sometimes at first sight I was a little bit nonplussed. But I cannot remember a single one of those visiting propagandists who did not quickly become a friend we enjoyed having with us.

I think most of our guests enjoyed themselves as much as we did. Mother would bustle around, serving us all with unquestioning cheerfulness. Father sat by the fire explaining the local situation. The arm-chair on the other side of the fireplace was for the visitor. My brother and I were quite satisfied with this arrangement. It left for us the corners of the fender-stool where we could sit with our backs to the warm grate and our eyes glued to the stranger. Very occasionally he would ignore our existence and the room would echo with strange, exciting words—Nietzsche, Dietzgen, dialectics, Engels, Hegel———. But more often he would turn to us with all the usual wiles of a grown-up trying to make friends with children.

I can recall only one serious misadventure in our attempts to make our guests feel at home. The redoubtable Dick Wallhead had arrived for a series of meetings. He was an ace among propagandists and we were delighted to have him. We had also heard that he was fond of music. My parents felt, therefore, that he must have the pleasure of listening to me play the piano.

I could play "Poet and Peasant", "Tannhäuser", "Il Trovatore", "Rigoletto", and at least a score of other pieces with deadly accuracy. I swear to the accuracy for Mr. Garvie who was blind and had a bookseller's shop in Cowdenbeath High Street, had given me very special facilities for practising.

In the parlour above his shop he had two pianos, an ordinary one and a mechanical one just like those in the ice-cream shops. He and I were very good friends and read together several volumes of *The Story of the Working Class throughout the Ages*. A group of Cowdenbeath Socialists had clubbed together to buy the series which at that time had quite a vogue. The books were stored in Mr. Garvie's backshop. He was an eager, intelligent man, with a great faith in education. I enjoyed reading to him and hearing his sharp

questions and criticisms. As an exchange in courtesies
he invited me to use his pianos. I would wind up the
mechanical one and, while it drummed out the scroll,
keep perfect time on the other.

In preparation for Dick Wallhead's visit our mother
moved the piano from the best parlour bedroom to our
kitchen-living-room. All was in readiness for our guest.
After supper was cleared away, my parents mildly
announced that he must hear me play. I was egged
on to begin.

Wallhead sat by the fire looking more and more
gloomy and disgruntled. I could feel antipathetic
currents of feeling swirling around the room. Finally,
able to bear it no longer, he spluttered out in his
cracked croak of a voice: "That girl can't play the
piano and never WILL be able to play."

I don't remember what happened immediately after
that. My parents must have felt a bit damped. To pay
for piano-lessons, examinations and all, was a big drain
on their tiny income. They had very great faith. My
own sympathies were divided. I dimly realized that
Wallhead was right. And I hated practising. Anyhow,
before the end of his visit we were all good friends.

In fairness I must say that that was the only time
when a guest had that kind of entertainment thrust on
him.

When visitors were due, our mother had us carefully
warned to sit quietly by the fire and go on working at
home-lessons, or reading our story-books so as not to
be a nuisance.

But there were regular old-timers who were special favourites with us and would not allow us to be quiet. James Maxton, for instance, would saunter in with a jaunty air and at once look challengingly around for someone to play with. At least that is how it seemed to us. His brother-in-law, the Rev. J. Munro, was another disrupter of the peace. Before he had been more than an hour in the house he had even my shy little brother on top of a chair shouting out Burns' poems. I was sorry he insisted on teaching him "Fair fa' your honest, sonsie face, great chieftain o' the puddin'-race", for I thought the "Address to a Haggis" the dullest poem Burns ever wrote. But my brother enjoyed it. "Tam Samson's Elegy" was more to my liking. Munro enchanted us for ever by the gusto with which he used to recite it, especially the way he intoned the last three words of every verse—"Tam Samson's deed!"[1]

A less boisterous, but painstaking guest was the Rev. Campbell Stephen. He had no gift for stories but, as we grew older, we found that he was hot stuff on quadratic equations.

As I changed from childhood to adolescence I looked forward with increasing eagerness to these week-end visitors. I was grateful to those who did not try to talk down to us; to those who answered our questions with the same gravity with which we asked them. Maxton would never do that. Always urbanely charming, and with a delightful sense of humour, he would answer nothing seriously. I would tenaciously stick to my point

[1] Dead.

as long as I could in spite of the charm and the humour. But in the end I was always turned away hungry and made to feel a fool for being so clumsily importunate.

As I grew older (I am now thinking of the years just after the war) it seemed a matter of life and death to have all sorts of questions answered.

The coalfields were in a ferment. The union had never been so strong and its morale was even stronger. Miners returning from active service joined in with the rest to demand better conditions. Hadn't the Government said that that was what the fighting had been about? To make life more spacious and gracious for the ordinary man? Lloyd George knew all the words. Our people were now bent on packing some content into them. Now was the time, father said. The sidings were empty. The returning soldiers were not in a mood to be played with. Every advantage lay with the miners.

The coal companies were in a state of funk. They knew the men were in a position to dictate terms. They saw themselves being compelled to disgorge some of the excessive wealth they had piled up during the war.

At this point the Government intervened, offering the Sankey Commission. The miners were to appoint half the commissioners, the coal companies the other half, and Sir J. Sankey was to act as chairman. It was a tempting offer. The more so as, in the same breath, the Government let it be understood that, if there was a national stoppage, soldiers would be drafted into the coalfields and any subsequent bloodshed would be upon the miners' own heads.

48

Our home, like thousands of others, rang with the controversy. To accept the commission and abide by its findings or to strike without delay and put the issue to a contest between the naked strength of miner and coal-owner?

Most of our lot were for striking. They did not trust Lloyd George. They did not trust any of the Government. They felt they would be tricked and they knew that by virtue of their own strength they could at that moment have wrung solid concessions from the coal companies.

The most powerful voice for accepting the commission was that of Bob Smillie. Bob we loved, trusted and respected. We knew he was incapable of deceiving us. Every phase of his life had been marked by lion-hearted endurance. At that time he was president of the M.F.G.B.[1] and at the height of his power. By the narrowest of margins the coalfields finally voted in favour of accepting the commission. Hurriedly an interim report was got out and the growling of the suspicious was drowned in promises of an immediate reduction of the working hours from eight to seven and some advance in wages. In addition, it soon became evident that Smillie, in his evidence before the commission, was putting an unanswerable case for the miners. Nationalization, a six-hour working-day, pit-head baths, improved wages, were just around the corner. The miners, to clinch matters, received the following letter from Bonar Law:

[1] Miners' Federation of Great Britain.

11, *Downing Street*,
Whitehall, S.W.,
21*st March*, 1919.

Dear Sir,

Speaking in the House of Commons last night I made a statement in regard to the Government policy in connection with the Report of the Coal Industry Commission. I have pleasure in confirming, as I understand you wish me to do, my statement that the Government are prepared to carry out in the spirit and the letter the recommendations of Sir John Sankey's Report.

Yours faithfully,

A. BONAR LAW.

We were getting on famously. It was an alive, bracing time. The union was strong. The I.L.P. was growing rapidly in numbers and influence. In our part of the world it was a close cordial fellowship proud of its anti-war record. It was succeeding so well that we forgot to remember, unless as good yarns to tell around the fireside, the harsher side of war-time treatment. It was quite true that many of our best people had been in gaol, that many more, such as my father, burned their calling-up papers and were not sent to prison by the mere accident of their occupations. There had, too, been many ugly incidents at meetings. But war memories faded very quickly. We were growing too fast to have time to look behind. Very soon now we would revolutionize the world. Our socialist hymns seemed to me to give a pretty good

50

idea of what it was all about. I could never sing in tune, but I mumbled fervently to myself the words of the songs we were taught to sing every Sunday forenoon in our socialist Sunday school.

"We are children but some day we'll be big and strong and say, none shall slave and none shall slay, comrades all together."

One of our favourite hymns seemed to me to contain the whole of history, and everything about the present and future that really mattered. It went something like this:

Lift up the people's banner, now trailing in the dust,
A million hands are ready to guard the sacred trust;
With steps that never falter and hearts that grow more
strong;
Till victory end our warfare we sternly march along.
Through ages of oppression, we bore the heavy load,
While others reaped the harvest from seeds the people
sowed;
Down in the earth we burrowed, or fed the furnace heats,
We felled the mighty forests, we built the mighty fleets.
But after bitter ages of hunger and despair
The slave has snapped his fetters and bids his foes beware.
We shall be slaves no longer, the nations soon shall know,
That all who live must labour and all who reap must
sow.
So on we march to battle, with souls that shall not rest,
Until the world we live in is by the world possessed.
And filled with perfect manhood, in beauty it shall move,
One heart, one home, one nation, whose king and lord is
love.

51

That sort of thing is not meant to be read in cold blood by grown-up people. They can see all its inadequacies. But our blood was warm, we were young, infinitely impressionable. Every line was real to us. "Down in the earth we burrowed" meant our fathers working in the pits right under our feet. We had lots of friends working in the shipyards along the Forth and Clyde. It was they who "built the mighty fleets". And some of our cousins and uncles and brothers who had emigrated to Canada were sure to be among those who "fell the mighty forests".

I was now completely captivated by the socialist movement and well on the way to becoming a youthful socialist edition of Colonel Blimp. I had my prejudices. I had no doubts. I had not the slightest inkling of what went on under the skin of people who did not see things exactly as I did. Idealism, ancestor worship and a happy feeling that we were the people who would one day revolutionize the world so that "none shall slave and none shall slay" seemed to me just about everything in philosophy, religion and economics that anyone need bother about.

One day, shortly after the war ended, my father announced that Clifford Allen was coming to stay with us. That was staggering news. Clifford Allen, a leading figure in the I.L.P. and in the No Conscription Fellowship, seemed to us the very embodiment of the martyrdom that some of our members had suffered during the war.

Before he arrived father told mother that he must

be given most-favoured-nation treatment. That meant having a fire kindled in his bedroom. For husky young fellows, mother thought that unnecessary. But when the propagandist was elderly or not too robust, this extra little privilege was arranged. Clifford Allen, we were gravely told, had had a severe prison sentence and as a result was very, very ill.

I curled up as usual on the corner of the fender-stool and waited tensely for the stranger to appear. A hero was visiting our home. Everyone said that he had not long to live. That his health had been ruined by prison. I had to wait a long time. The local I.L.P. Committee had met the train and they had all gone directly to the hall. Half-way through the evening someone came in with the news that the meeting was a complete fiasco. Something had gone wrong with the timing or advertising and, anyhow, it was a Saturday evening, the hardest of all nights to assemble a crowd. I was wrung with pity. To think that a dying man had dragged himself all the way from London to Cowdenbeath only to be met by such callous indifference.

I settled myself for another long wait. At last I heard the front door opening and knew that the speaker, my father and the rest of the I.L.P. Committee were treading along the lobby towards the kitchen door. By the time the door opened, my eyes were hazy with excitement. I shall never forget the tall, ascetic face and figure of Clifford Allen framed in our kitchen doorway with half a dozen squat dark-looking miners grouped around him. I should not have been surprised if he had suddenly sprouted wings and a halo.

Later in the evening, when everyone else had gone he won our hearts all over again by telling us how in prison he and another conscientious objector played an intricate game of chess, one move being made each day by signing to one another when as prisoners they were assembled and marched round and round the exercise-yard. It was all very elevating. Ours was a wonderful movement. All knights in shining armour who would never rest until the words in the songs of our socialist hymn-books had indeed come to pass.

I was wild with impatience when I thought of how much of this struggle I had already missed. I had been born so late that I could not even be a suffragette.

Mrs. Helen Crawfurd, one of the old militant group, sometimes stayed with us as a visiting I.L.P. propagandist. Responding to our eager prompting, she would talk for hours about her window-breaking adventures and prison exploits. I longed to have broken windows and been sent to prison for the greater power and glory of the suffragette cause, and wondered ruefully if anything at all would be left to do by the time I had finished with school.

It was Grandfather Lee who cheered me most when I was in this mood. "Lass," he would say, "there will be plenty left for you to do. It takes longer than you think."

CHAPTER IV

I FOUND it a great nuisance when I had to begin to think about earning a living. I felt no special urge to stand behind a shop counter all day or to sit typing in an office or to join the early morning rush of girls waiting for the tram to take them to the Dunfermline factories.

But my father and mother were quietly insistent. I was fourteen. The time had come when I must prove that my feet were on solid ground, that I knew what I wanted to do.

There was a vague notion floating around the family that I ought to take a course in "business training"! I was not enthusiastic.

In the end we agreed that I might remain at school for one year more. But, as a gesture to a wage-earning future, I was at the same time to attend night-school classes in shorthand and book-keeping.

When my fifteenth birthday arrived I had quite definitely decided that I did not want to leave school. That was awkward for my parents. They were willing enough for me to continue; but fearful about incurring expenses they could not meet.

The examination results decided the issue. I had

taken first place in class. Mother was determined that I should go on. Blindly determined. She, who always liked to plan her way so carefully embarked on this grave undertaking without the least idea as to where the money was to come from. She would carry me on as far as she could. She was game. Something might turn up.

That year, with a view to assisting Providence, she put a shilling each way on the Derby. We teased her mercilessly when we found out about this. My father was strictly opposed to gambling in every form. Mother knew this and, as always, agreed with him. But she was bent on helping me to do the things I had set my heart on. Somehow or other I had to be put through secondary school and then through college. She was willing even to risk sinning a little if that would help.

The following year I found it not so easy to keep grinding away at school work. I did only indifferently well. I was at the age when you parade arm-in-arm along the school corridors with one eye on your books and the other on the look-out for mischief. Beath Secondary was a large mixed school. I should have hated it to have been anything else. Schools exclusively for girls struck me as silly; especially when later on we had to compete against men students in University classes. It was more reassuring to have to scramble for your place in a mixed examination list. We, at least, knew where we stood.

And I rather imagine that there was less furtiveness

and romanticism among us than appears to haunt adolescent school life where boys and girls are educated entirely apart. We were just ordinary, healthy youngsters reaching an age when to be shyly flirtatious was as inevitable as breathing. Sometimes when we ought to have been entirely preoccupied with conjugating *amo, amas, amat*, we were wondering instead what it was all about.

That was one cause of indifferent examination results. The other, and the obvious one to my father and mother was that I was giving too much time to socialist activities. On Sunday forenoon there was the socialist Sunday school. On Sunday evening there were the great public meetings. On Saturday there was the arrival of the visiting propagandist. And, at least two nights during the week there were the I.L.P. dues to collect. It was my particular job to go from door to door every week, visiting each member of the Cowdenbeath I.L.P., collecting his or her membership dues and stamping the membership card. I loved doing this. Almost every house of call made me one of the family. Sometimes I would stop and have tea. Much too often we would argue for hours when I ought to have been more business-like and hurrying on to the other doors.

Besides politics I was greatly concerned at this time about religion. My grandfather was a devoutly religious man of simple unquestioning faith. My father held that religion was an exploded myth. I loved and respected both men so had to turn to and wrestle with the question for myself. The bookshelves of my friends

57

were loaded with explosive material. I picked up Ingersol, Tom Paine, Joseph McCabe, a score of tracts written by the pamphleteers of the rationalist press and even that monstrous Big Bertha among this kind of literature, *Li Hung Chang's Scrap Book*. Stunned and overborne by the pressure of these polemics, I thrust all the books aside and told myself I had better think things out for myself.

I became violently anti-sectarian. I wept for Hypatia, torn limb from limb by the early Christians. I could see with horrible visual precision the tortured bodies of victims of the Inquisition. I could hear the screams of harmless old women burned as witches by the Kirk Elders in my own native Scotland as recently as 1722. That was bringing it very near home. It seemed to me that the original Christian had had some sense of pity, but that the sects that later on used his name had none at all.

I did not get much beyond that. Even in my childish gropings I rejected the simple anthropomorphic view of God. At five I had been able to visualize Santa Claus with red gown, white beard, reindeer sledge and all. But at fifteen, I could not quite see God as a benevolent bearded gentleman living above the clouds and made in the image of man. It had to be something a little less concrete than that. Perhaps there was something in the pantheistic view of the universe. I discovered Wordsworth's "Tintern Abbey" and took what refuge I could from a bleakly mechanistic view of life in the lines:

And I have felt
A presence that disturbs me with the joy
Of elevated thoughts; a sense sublime
Of something far more deeply interfused,
Whose dwelling is the light of setting suns,
And the round ocean, and the living air,
And the blue sky, and in the mind of man:
A motion and a spirit, that impels
All thinking things, all objects of all thought,
And rolls through all things.

After carefully looking up the dictionary to confirm that agnostic meant "I do not know", I decided that so far as I could label myself I appeared to be a cross between a pantheist and an agnostic.

I was a bit sensitive about the untidiness of such a position especially when arguing with those of my friends who were bright clear Marxist materialists, but I could not for the life of me see my way through to anything more presentable.

My mother was always uneasy when we discussed religion. I could never quite make out whether piety or prudence accounted for her reactions. Neither then nor now would she allow us to use God's name lightly. Why go out of our way to make another enemy, seemed to be her point of view, when we were already exposed on every front in our fights with coal companies and political time-servers.

Going from door to door collecting the I.L.P. dues, I could have arguments about politics and religion in every other household. But I could not hope to make much headway with school work. I had to choose between arguing about God and the Devil and Engels and Joseph Dietzgen, and passing my school examinations.

I cannot imagine either of my parents being harsh or nagging. They left me entirely to my own devices. But I knew they were worrying. No tyranny could have been as effective as that. In a violent reaction, after a period of slacking, I made a foolish vow. I made a pact with myself that I would be ready to leave for the University at the end of my fifth year and that I would become Dux of the school before leaving.

Lord, how I worked: every night, cram, cram, cram. Every other thought and activity banished. There was no more reading for fun, or dreaming or debating from door to door. The world, as the school year dragged slowly on, became one long nightmare of examinations. I had my little triumph and took first place in school then, a few weeks later, broke down completely.

We had reached that waiting time at school when all the examinations are over but the end of the term still some weeks ahead. The teachers were mercifully easy on us. Only the minimum of routine tasks were imposed. But even that had become too much for me. One warm day in the Latin class I found I could no longer see. The words were all blurred and made no sense. I always hated Latin. I was bad at it and it never, at the best of times, made much sense to me. But now my strength was spent. I lurched forward on the desk weeping uncontrollably.

That last year at school I worked harder than at any

other time in my life. It left me with a sour distaste of cramming. I made up my mind that when I went to the University I would allow myself to sprawl a bit. I would have to be careful to get through my examinations. But I was determined not to get strung up on the rack of competing for first place in any of my classes.

Actually what happened was that in the early part of the University term I did very little work, but, as examination time drew near, I crammed with the best. I was too scared of failing to maintain my cavalier attitude right through. This got me a first-class certificate in all classes except one. The exception was economic history. I had blithely decided that as I was doing more general reading on that subject than on any other there was no need for me to memorize, parrot fashion, the lectures read out to us in class. That was a mistake. I got only a Second and had all my cynicism about the examination system confirmed. It just didn't do to get interested in a subject. That tempted you to read too widely. The recipe for successful results was very simple. Find out anything your lecturer had written, memorize copious notes of lectures, and cultivate the art of emptying out on to the examination paper everything you knew from these sources grouped in some sort of order around the actual questions asked.

The novelty subject for me in my first University year was psychology. I was fascinated by all the new words. Nothing like it had happened to me since the

61

time I sat on the corner of the fender-stool listening to my father's friends discuss Dietzgen, Nietzsche, dialectics, eclectics, the proletariat and the bourgeoisie.

I broke my usual rule and, in addition to the prescribed books read everything of Havelock Ellis and of Freud that I could lay hands on. Considering my erudition, I am bound to laugh at two incidents that occurred that same year.

One day, going along Princes Street, I caught sight of a familiar face. I recognized a girl from home and ran careering along the street to catch up with her. She was a very great swell, fur-coat and powder and paint to the eyes. I knew her home people. They were one of the poorest miners' families in the place. I was a little bit surprised by her grandeur, but she was a girl I had always liked and I was glad to see her and, anyhow, I did not get things connected up any more than that. She seemed taken aback for a moment when I grabbed her arm, but I hauled her along towards the nearest tea shop and said we must have a cup of tea together. That would be fine, she said, "but if you will just wait here I must go round the corner first." I waited and she came back quite soon, smiling radiantly.

We had tea together and she insisted on paying for both. I met her several times afterwards and always enjoyed her company. I had not the least inkling of what must have been so plain to the rest of the world. Her profession was exactly what you may have guessed it to be.

Years later, when she was dying and there could be

no more dissembling, I met her again. Rallying some of her old verve, she sat up in bed and began to laugh. It was then she told me that when I had first run after her in Princes Street, she had not had "a penny to bless herself with", so she had dashed round to a familiar pawnshop "to raise the wind". She was not going to be affronted by having a "kid" pay for her tea.

Another time, as I was walking towards my lodgings rather late in the day, a rather good-looking man of about fifty lifted his hat and said "good evening" to me. I at once said "good evening" and we fell into step. I had no idea who he was, but I would on no account have hurt his feelings by telling him so. I had often been in this predicament in Fifeshire. All sorts of people knew my family and would greet us as we passed. I was hopeless at remembering faces. But this was Edinburgh, not Cowdenbeath. When we reached the quiet of the Meadows behind Edinburgh Infirmary my friend began to be demonstrative in his affection. I quite suddenly realized what was happening. I had been "picked up" and had not known it. I was abjectly apologetic and sorry for making the man look so foolish. Then it all seemed so funny that I almost choked as I hurried away. I was trying not to laugh out loud.

So much for my worldly wisdom. I had not recognized the most obvious type of street-walker (not that it would have mattered; I liked the girl), nor known when I was being "picked up". But from my text-books I had assembled a most unholy collection of words. They stood me in good stead when examination time came round. I got a first-class certificate in psychology.

The following year—my second in Edinburgh—some of us had little time for study until the term was well begun. We had a rectorial election on hand. Bertrand Russell was Labour candidate. We had invited him, nominated him and now had to see the thing through.

I was overawed by the thought of what we had undertaken; but reassured by the worldly air of one or two of the older students. The only thing to do, apparently, was to put one's best foot forward and try to look as wise as the rest.

Our biggest effort was the production of a paper which we were bound to sell instead of giving away in the traditional manner of the richer student parties. After much heart-searching, the name we found for the paper was *Rebel Student*. We thought it a pretty distinguished production, but had difficulty in selling a sufficient number of copies to clear the printer's bill.

An emergency meeting had to be called to consider the financial crisis. Stacks of *Rebel Students* looked up at us inquiringly from the floor of the committee-room. We had exhausted our market among the student population. There was only one thing left to do. We must each take a bundle of papers and go out into the town and sell them. That sounds easy. But have you ever tried selling papers for the first time? I felt

my legs unaccountably weak. I put it off as long as I
could. But postponement did not help. There lay the
papers; they had to be sold.

I taunted myself with my cowardice. What was
the use of pretending to be a revolutionary if I was
afraid even to take a bundle of papers under my arm
and go out into the streets and sell them? After all, it
might be worse. Think of our socialist hymn ". . . come
dungeons dark or gallows grim . . . " In the end I
took up my post outside Pringle's Picture Palace,
hoping to catch the crowd that poured into the great
Sunday-night meetings that the Communist Party
held there at that time. And I found it was true what
everyone had said. Getting started was the worst.
There seemed dozens of other newsvendors shouting
their wares: "*Sunday Worker*, one penny"—"*Labour
Monthly*, sixpence"—"*Russia To-day*, twopence". I
got started at last: "*Rebel Student*, two-pence; *Rebel
Student*, two-pence!" The more nervous I became the
louder I shouted. I had a disagreeable sensation of
tears in the offing. That would have been a fine thing
for a revolutionary. So I shouted louder still, and began
to do good business. Many of the crowd stopped to buy.
They were a rough-and-ready, sympathetic lot. Some
smiled to me; some smiled at me. I was too tensely
poised to notice much. But for one moment, I happened to look behind. A shy, gentle-natured girl
student had been told off along with me to sell papers
at this same stance. I caught sight of her, a bundle of
papers under one arm, clutching a brass railing in the

F   65

hall entrance with the other, head thrown back, white to the lips, mutely repeating "*Rebel Student*", but never a sound coming out, and no customers!

Socialist activities were once again taking more of my time than I could afford. I was drifting into the same sort of dangerous muddle that I had got into during my fourth year at school. And again I was blackmailed into a bout of hard work by the gentle tolerance of my home people. I knew that although I went back to them with a wasted year behind me there would be no reproaches. That made the prospect too terrible. I decided I had better have an orgy of "swotting". My prize for good behaviour was the winning of £100 in a competitive examination in Roman Law and Constitutional History and Law.

The money was badly needed. I was beginning to see signs of strain at home. My mother was up to every dodge to keep me from noticing anything. I was bookish and absent-minded. But there was a limit even to *my* blindness.

I have often been asked how it was possible for a working miner to pay for university training for his daughter. That makes coal-mining sound a very profitable occupation. It worked out something like this. I leave you to judge for yourself.

Under the Fife Education Authority, I had more help given to me than I would have had almost anywhere else in Great Britain. That was one of the by-products of a lively socialist movement in the industrial parts of Fife. Years before I was born, Grandfather Lee and a handful of others of his generation were already members of the old school boards. Steadily they pressed for free books, better schools, free secondary education, maintenance grants for all. "Education", Grandfather Lee was fond of saying, "was a grand thing".

We laughed lovingly at some of his dreams. He himself was taught to read and write by his sons. He had great faith in what a younger generation, able to recite the principles of Archimedes and to speak bad French, would one day do for their people.

By the time I was old enough for school, a small part of the socialist programme had been won. At eleven years of age we finished with the elementary school; those who did sufficiently well in the examinations had the option of going on to the secondary school.

If our parents could manage to feed and clothe us, the education authority did the rest. Free books and schooling were provided right to the point when we were ready to leave for college or university. Those pupils who had to travel any distance to the secondary school had their bus or train fares paid for.

When I was ready to leave for Edinburgh University, Fife Education Authority presented me with a maintenance allowance of forty-five pounds per year. In addition, the Carnegie Trust paid half my class fees. I was left to find the other half, money for essential text-books, lodgings, meals and clothing. There were a number of hostels where it was usual for women students to live. These were too expensive for me.

For which I was thankful! I hated regimentation and much preferred a room I found for fourteen shillings a week.

Paying for a warm midday meal was the thing I grudged most. My total living expenses had to be kept under thirty shillings a week. I would rather have had no lunch than do without coffee in the middle of the morning, and, if any good movie or show came to town, I liked seeing it. There was only one way of budgeting for that kind of extravagance. I made my main meal most days of soup, fourpence, apple dumpling, or any other sweet that was sufficiently filling, another fourpence. Sometimes, for variety, I cut out the soup and had a fourpenny meat roll instead. I did not mind much what I ate and could digest almost anything.

In the mornings and evenings I concocted a meal in my lodgings. These too cost very little for every week a hamper arrived from home with tea, homemade cake and scones, sometimes eggs, sometimes home-made potted meat and always, even at times of economic depression at home much greater than I realized, funny little packets stuffed in the corners with chocolate or cheap sweets.

I was enjoying life and had no complaints. I was well protected too against the sharp, biting Edinburgh winds by an adequate supply of warm clothing. I was not exactly a model of fashion, but what of that! Considering the *tour de force* with which I had been assembled, I was mighty well pleased.

Even the simplest college outfit costs an unconscionable amount of money. My mother had been almost at her wits' end to know how we were to clear that particular hurdle. We had no reserves in the bank. We traded almost exclusively with the Co-operative Society, where no credit was allowed.

Then, one day, inspiration came. Greatly daring, mother made up her mind. Clothes I had to have and clothes she was going to get for me. With the light of battle in her eyes, she marched down Cowdenbeath High Street towards Forrests, one of the best drapery stores in town. During the war years, when money had been a little more plentiful, Forrests had developed a less blatantly shoddy line of goods than has usually to be stocked in mining communities where cheapness above all must be considered. "Their stuff was dear," mother said, "but good."

So, pocketing her pride and the habits of a lifetime she went to Forrests and asked if she could be allowed to "take on". She need have had no fear. Tradespeople in that size of town know their public. She was cordially invited to help herself to whatever she wanted. Payment could come later.

Every day for about a week she came staggering home with her parcels. I got two costumes, two blouses, a jersey, an overcoat, stockings, handkerchiefs, and even a bright blue velveteen afternoon dress with silver lace draped over the skirt.

One of the parcels I opened gave me a violent shock. I wondered if my good, sensible mother had gone stark, staring mad.

On top was a voluminous white nightgown of the best Irish linen, elaborately embroidered, complete with long, tight sleeves and a cape. Underneath there were bloomers drawn in tightly at the knees and adorned with frills and pale-blue ribbons. There was also a chemise and a camisole of equally elaborate design. The stuff must have cost a fortune. And this was 1922, the very height of the pyjama age. I would rather have died than be caught by fellow-students floating around in an outfit of that kind. I was staggered and didn't know whether to laugh or cry. My mother's face was the last straw. She was looking at me in a non-committal kind of way, veering towards a smile.

This, she explained, was her special present to me. No, it had not come from Forrests. It had come from a box beneath her bed. It had been sent to her from Dublin by Dr. Body and his wife (friends of the old Arcade days) as a wedding present. But that, I protested, was twenty-two years ago. Yes, she agreed, so it was. But I could see for myself that the stuff was as good as new. It had been worn only once, then laid away for a rainy day.

By such varied means I was ultimately launched. The worst time was towards the end of my third year. Someone told me that if I could produce a respectable array of class certificates and prove need as well, I might be able to get an extra grant from the Carnegie Trust. I was not very sanguine about that but did as directed. In reply, a letter came asking me to call on a certain Mr. Burns in his Dunfermline office.

I went to the appointment in a highly-strung, defiant state of mind. What sort of questions would I be asked? Would I be humiliated more than I could bear? Perhaps make an ass of myself by breaking down during the interview. We were proud people. It was my parents' code that they had never begged nor borrowed and had always paid their way. That was before mining families had been humbled by long years of unemployment, means tests, and public assistance committees.

I decided to stand for just so much and no more. But I need not have feared. A courteous official shook hands with me, sent to the next room for a file where, apparently, he had all the particulars he needed, then, within a few minutes, was again shaking hands and I found myself leaving the office with twenty brand new Scotch pound notes stuffed into my handbag.

Soon after that I got another windfall. I won the £100 prize in the Law examination. Then, in my fourth year, I got a half share in a £20 prize in the Education class. As the Fife Authority did not reduce my yearly grant of £45 because of prize money (for a bit I lived in terror of that happening), in my last few terms at Edinburgh I was comparatively opulent.

Another change at home still further reduced the strain. My brother was now seventeen and eager to be allowed to go to Australia. A Government agent had been touring the mining district with a magic lantern show, illustrating the glorious life that awaited young men who were prepared to emigrate.

71

My brother was fascinated. He plunged into a romantic fantasy in which he was already riding a horse in the wide open spaces and driving the cattle home to the ranch.

My parents said he was too young to go so far away from home. They were strongly against the idea. But he had set his heart on it. One term, when I came home from college, he was waiting for me to intercede for him. Could I not persuade father and mother that it was a good idea? I thought about it a great deal. We were passionately attached to one another. The thought of his leaving for the other end of the world was like the wrench of losing a limb. But what was there for him to do if he remained at home? He had not wanted to continue at school and had no special liking or talent for school work. We all of us regarded work down the pit as a last resort, the thing he must be saved from if at all possible.

For almost three years he had been working in the office of a linen factory in Dunfermline. He earned £1 a week and had heavy travelling expenses deducted from that. What was left for the sort of things for which a young fellow likes to have money to burn? How could he have enough in his pocket to take a pretty girl to the Palais de Danse on a Saturday night? Or to join sports clubs, or to do anything at all? He was a bundle of wants and discontents. Once when we were both clamouring for the impossible in the thoughtless way of seventeen and twenty, our mother turned on us, almost angry. "I wish you were still bairns," she said. "I could manage you then. That was your happiest time." Father, hearing this, looked up from his paper with a twinkle in his eye and retorted, "*Your* happiest time, you mean."

Every Monday evening a regular pantomime worked itself out. My brother, home from work and ready to go out to meet his pals, would stand in the doorway, making signals of distress towards mother. His Saturday pocket-money was spent. He was again broke. Mother would make angry answering gestures whose meaning could not be misunderstood. Not a word would be spoken. My father and I, reading quietly by the fireside, would wink at one another. The rules of the game were that we were supposed to be entirely unaware of what was going on. In the end, mother would follow my brother to the outside door, thrust a sixpence into his hand muttering fiercely as she did so that this was the very last time that she would give in to him. The following Monday the same pantomime would be staged with entirely the same results.

I wondered how it was all going to end. The decay that had begun to invade the mining industry had already overtaken the linen trade.

Australia was a younger country. I knew very little about it. But going there was at least a gamble that might lead to quite a good life. My brother's health was what finally decided me. He was now a husky young fellow chafing at the restrictions of an office-stool. But, after the sanatorium period in his childhood, we never felt quite certain about him. Ours was a damp, cold climate. Australia might give him a better chance of a healthy life. Our decision had to be made quickly. We had no money for steamship passages. The Government was offering to send boys out to Australia for £2, provided they were under eighteen years of age.

Mother, looking very sad, at last had to yield to him. She began to prepare for his departure. Her son must not go out into the world without a good stock of durable clothing. Once again she had to ask Forrest if she might "take on" a little. She hated asking for credit. It always worried her, and it was against her principles. But our needs came before everything else.

One day during term-time I saw my brother leave from Edinburgh station. He was a great, hopeful young fellow, the rest of his luggage off in advance but hugging his violin. He never would practise much but he had a certain facility for playing and was boastfully pleased with the name inside the instrument. It had been made by Alexander Greig, his own great-uncle. My good-bye present was a canvas and leather outside cover for his fiddle.

We made a pact with one another that no matter what happened he would write regularly to our mother saying everything was fine, but that he would write under separate cover to me saying bluntly and truthfully, just exactly what was happening to him.

CHAPTER V

IF I could have afforded it when I left school, I would have gone to Oxford or Cambridge. That seemed the dazzlingly splendid thing to do. But now I know the south I am rather glad that I had to choose either Edinburgh or St. Andrews. The southern counties are very lovely. But in such a flat, enervatingly peaceful kind of way! There are no Pentland Hills within easy reach of Oxford or Cambridge, and no Arthur's Seat dumped right at the College gate.

I liked living in Edinburgh. It has lots of slums like the rest of our cities and no one could call it a gay, colourful place. But, for all that, in its own sober, northern way, it has great beauty and distinction. At eighteen, with the drab unloveliness of colliery districts as my standard of comparison, I found it very pleasant to be living there.

I liked trailing around the town. I liked still more the times when we were free for the whole day and could go off on tramps over the hills. And I am undyingly grateful to the Carnegie Public Library on George IV Bridge.

But of the University itself what is there to be said? It was the least important part of student life for me.

In saying that I am not trying to be smart or facetious. I am too anxious to set down as candidly as I know how the influences that formed my point of view and selected my subsequent activities. Why I feel driven to do this will, I hope, become clear in the later chapters of this book. But, for the moment, I think I had better resist the temptation to argue and simply describe incidents and impressions as I happen to recall them.

I spent term-time in Edinburgh and the long College vacations at home. Crossing from Edinburgh to the coalfields on the northern side of the Forth was, in a physical sense, like moving from a brightly-lit room into semi-darkness. But, emotionally and intellectually, it was for me exactly the other way round. At that time there was a vigorous socialist movement in the industrial parts of Fife. In odd corners of this movement there were men whose knowledge of industrial history, economics and philosophy made me ashamed of how little I knew. Theirs was an eager, questioning purposeful kind of knowledge; in exhilarating contrast to the dead, disconnected, parroting that earned us our University degrees. Of course, the comparisons I made were grossly biassed. I contrasted the average university student with the exceptional collier. I am not pretending otherwise. But at the time that never occurred to me. I was too exuberantly partisan, and too elated at the thought of what our socialist movement stood for and what it was going to do.

It was a dull business returning from heated arguments on how to make the whole world anew to the factory routine of swotting for examinations. Each term I returned to Edinburgh with increasing reluctance. The novelty of the place had worn off. It did not answer or even ask any of the questions that I was most concerned about. But I was in honour bound to plod steadily on until I had collected the certificates I needed as a preliminary to earning my living.

The strictly utilitarian part of University life consisted of going in droves to one class after another, taking down copious notes of lectures, memorizing these and reading the prescribed books.

At certain times of the year we poured out all we could remember on to our examination papers. Given a reasonable mixture of industry and luck, this process earned us pass certificates. Once these were safely netted we could comfortably forget all but the vaguest medley of what we had memorized and settle down to "swot up" some other subject.

At the end of four and a half years of that sort of thing I had assembled an M.A. degree, a teacher's certificate, a diploma in education and, as a final flourish, an LL.B. degree. That was considered pretty good going so it was probably foolish of me to have a feeling of guilt about it all. But it did seem an awful fraud to possess for life a barrow-load of certificates, knowing all the time just how very little the whole performance signified.

I don't know quite what I expected from a university. Certainly something a little less reach-me-down than the degree-collecting process turned out to be.

One or two of our professors lectured with a freshness and enthusiasm that, looking back on, I can appreciate now better than I did then.

Old Professor Grierson of the English department, for instance, had a warm, infectious intensity that few of us could resist. Apparently undismayed by the rows upon rows of us, he would abandon himself to a favourite author, declaiming from selected passages for a solid hour on end with all the ardour of a young lover for a new-found love.

We were all on our best behaviour in the old man's classroom, for we liked him, and those who by temperament were unable to share his enthusiasms, at least marvelled at them. I boggled a bit over some of his Wordsworth but, otherwise, was one of his most impressionable disciples.

Professor Harvey Littlejohn was another of our lecturers who was never dull. His subject was forensic medicine. He talked of crime and criminals with a relish that, if we had been older and less grateful for any kind of entertainment, we might have been inclined to deprecate. Certainly his was a very extraordinary personality. As he lectured he dramatized each crime, acting now the part of the murderer, now the victim. It was like being back in the old Arcade Theatre watching a rattling good melodrama.

But most of our lecturers were dreary and circumspect. I suppose they had to be in order to survive.

Edinburgh is not the sort of place to encourage any kind of unorthodoxy.

Only one of them during the four and a half years I attended classes made any attempt to break away from the mechanical routine. This incident, so far as I was concerned blew the gaff on the whole business.

I was then in my fourth year and had enrolled for a post-graduate course in education. This class was intended chiefly for those of us who expected to earn our living as teachers.

Professor Godfrey Thomson, newly-appointed to the Chair of Education, had just arrived in Edinburgh, apparently bringing with him a rather high opinion of Scottish standards of education.

We trooped into his introductory lecture, produced our note-books and pencils, and settled down as usual to an hour's industrious note-taking.

Straight away the professor gave us an uncomfortable jog. We were to put away our note-books and pencils. They would not be needed. He did not intend reading aloud to us at dictation pace. It really was not necessary. The material we may have expected to have read out lecture by lecture was at our disposal in book form. This said, smiling in the friendliest way, he paused for a moment. The poor devil may even have expected some sign of approval. Instead there was mutiny in the air. Not noisy mutiny. Just sullen, anxious dismay. No notes? What did that mean? How then could we memorize our pieces in readiness for examination time? His next announcement was a

79

degree worse. We were to form ourselves into groups, each group doing a special piece of reading and research and, later in the term, reporting to the general class.

That was too much. That was taking the ground from under our feet altogether. That made the range of possible questions when examination time arrived too dangerously varied and unpredictable.

A few of us were flattered by the new professor's expectations and disgusted with the timidity of the bulk of the students. A fine showing it seemed to us, we made. Final-year students, most of us already in possession of at least one university degree and frightened out of our wits when a university class threatened to become anything more serious than memorizing set pieces taken down to dictation.

For once in my life I found myself on the side of authority. And, of course, I had to choose an occasion when authority was hopelessly outnumbered. The rebels won. The proposed scheme of work was modified substantially to give a much larger dose of formal lecturing than had been originally intended.

As far as I could discover the explanation of all this was simply fear. Economic fear. We were mostly poor students. We could not afford to take risks. We wanted to be left to plod along after the manner of the ancient Chinese in a kind of memory marathon race. We wanted the old familiar well-established system that enabled us, by sheer donkey work, to graduate successfully in the shortest possible time. Not to mince matters, our degrees were primarily our meal tickets.

Into this dim little, trim little world crashed the General Strike of May 1926. Very few students had any idea of what it was all about. Only a handful (at the outset) had any active animus against the miners.

But the University authorities, wasting no time about it, wholeheartedly began the task of turning each and all of us into bellicose class warriors. Students were encouraged (and bribed with the offer of easy money) to enlist as strike breakers.

Inside twenty-four hours I began to hear normally good-natured young fellows talk with unholy glee of the pleasure it would give them to run a tank through some of our mining villages.

I noted this, taken by surprise a bit. In theory I had always claimed that moods change rapidly, and in pretty much the same way, and to pretty much the same degree everywhere, when working people make any serious organized attempt to improve their economic position. I was impatient with people who argued that the British were different from the rest of the world; more good-natured and easy-going. It seemed to me entirely a matter of the degree of provocation. But, although in theory I knew all these arguments, emotionally I was unprepared. That is a common failing among socialists.

Apparently members of the General Council of the Trade Union Movement had not realized what they were up against any more than I had. Under their leadership, the working-class blundered into a general strike. During the whole of 1925 the coalowners and

G   81

the Government had been preparing elaborate strike-breaking machinery, the coalowners enjoying a special subsidy the while. Everyone knew these preparations were being made. Everyone knew a clash was imminent and inevitable. But the socialist movement, as it has done so often before and since, took its leaders on trust. It assumed that they had some sort of plan and knew what they were about. Actually, the Government and the coalowners, as in 1919 and 1921, found us easy game. Once again we had simply plunged blindly forward; and under such leadership, or lack of it if you like, disaster inevitably followed.

Rank-and-file workers all over the country proved magnificent scrappers. That always is true and always will be so, but of itself is not enough to win a war.

When the strike began a few of us from the University rushed down to the trade union headquarters to ask how we could help. I was given the job of receiving and dispatching orders for strike bulletins. We supplied the whole of Edinburgh and most of the surrounding districts. By the third or fourth day everything was going with a swing. We settled down for the duration and were blissfully pleased with life.

Then came the terrible news. The strike had been called off. Nothing had been won, yet the strike had been called off. Our leaders had run away. Ordinary men and women all over the country were standing their corner. But what good was that? Our leaders had intended perhaps only to make a mild industrial demonstration. Or had hoped that the mere threat of a general strike would be enough. The Government had called their bluff.

That evening, while the Central Strike Committee attended to the last funereal rites on the floor above us, we younger ones were huddled together in a corner of our improvised office, stunned and listless, demoralized by the utter, absolute fiasco of it all. We ended the day with a cursing competition. I was shocked at the language I suddenly discovered I knew.

Over the wireless, Baldwin, then Prime Minister, promised there would be no victimization. That was another joke. Such government assurances meant nothing at all. Men and women were victimized in every corner of Great Britain. Some of them have not even now been reinstated.

In the next few days I discovered that, although in Edinburgh the strike was over, in Fife my home people were still holding out. So were the miners everywhere. They were not running away. They were standing their ground even if they had to stand alone. I was torn between pride and pity. I longed to go home. But I dared not leave my books. In June, the following month, I had to sit my finals for my M.A. degree and for my teacher's certificate.

That was a nightmare time. I worked with what seemed to be a dark veil all around me. What was happening? Why had the other unions deserted us? How were they managing in Fife? What prospect was there of winning with such odds against us? Was it going to be a long battle? Would the women be able to stand it? Always when there are rumours of a strike but nothing is as yet definite, the women in the mining towns are more fearful than the men. But, invariably, once the battle is joined their staying power puts all waverers to shame.

At last I could go home. It was June. Examinations were over. I was qualified to teach if I could find work when the schools reopened in the autumn. But, for the present, there were more important things to be done.

That summer was one unceasing round of meetings. At all hours of the day and night we would dash off to corners of the coalfields where there was any sign or rumour of weakening morale. A group of boys or young men would go from street to street ringing a bell or beating a drum then shouting out their message: "A meeting—will be held—in the Welfare Hall—at three o'clock—this afternoon—speakers are——" and so on.

I enjoyed it all. In Edinburgh before I was free to go home I had been moody and dejected. But, once in the fight, there was no more time for moods. It is always that way. People's spirits rise once they get into action. Melancholy is very much the emotion of the onlooker.

The last months of the 1926 strike (lock-out we were meticulously careful to say) was a time of mounting anxiety. Our minds knew what our emotions refused to admit. The guns were all in the hands of the enemy. None of *their* women and children had to starve. They could hold out indefinitely. On our side, there was a limit to the food and funds we could collect. And beyond that, what?

One day some of our old friends and neighbours from Cowdenbeath (we had moved two miles to Lochgelly, to be nearer my father's work) made a proposal to me. They wanted me to go to Ireland to collect money for their soup-kitchen. All the surrounding districts had been bled white. More money had to be got from somewhere. I was doubtful about Ireland. Miners' bands had already gone there and were not doing too well. But I was willing enough to try, so I crossed Scotland to Stranraer and set sail for Belfast.

Once there I found that the only way of raising money was by street-corner meetings. There was terrific opposition. We bawled ourselves hoarse shouting above the din of the drums that the Oranch Lodges brought out against us.

The authorities would not allow collections to be taken, so I auctioned my stock of miners' lamps and, when these gave out, my friends raked in their cupboards and under their beds for every old pamphlet they could find on politics, economics, religion, or anything else under the sun. Those we sold at the meetings. No one wanted the antiquated pamphlets but many wanted to help the miners. It was an open conspiracy with the crowd to keep within the law.

In Dublin I got on better. But only after a difficult start. I had been told to go to Liberty Hall and present my credentials to Jim Larkin. Before ever I had time to produce them, this great towering figure of a man looked over the counter at me and snorted his contempt. No, he would not fix up meetings. "All right, all right," I said. "You have had your chance. You won't get it again."

Out I stamped. I had as hair-trigger nerves as he had. If we had been carrying revolvers, we would probably have shot one another on sight.

I went now to the headquarters of the postal workers and was immediately on good terms. They would co-operate with other unions and fix up meetings. Straight off, as a token of their fraternal feelings, they signed a cheque for twenty pounds.

In my anger I had left my suitcase at Larkin's office. I went back for it and was astonished at the change in the atmosphere. Larkin's assistant—he never had colleagues; he did not understand the meaning of the word—came forward at once to receive me. There had been an awful mistake. They did not know I had official credentials from the Fife Miners' Union. Larkin did not know that I was the granddaughter of his old friend, Michael Lee. No, sir, there was much too much, I told them, they did not know, and I was not playing. They begged and expostulated. They now had plans for meetings. They invited me to accept the hospitality of one of their members. Larkin came in as we were talking. He left his henchmen to do the explaining and apologizing and stood with his back to us. But I could see that he was listening attentively. I looked again at the big, powerful, helpless-looking figure and softened. All right. I would do their meetings. Larkin and I became good friends. He even un-

86

bent so far as to invite me once to go with him to a concert. It was an amateur affair held somewhere in the rear of his office buildings. We had been seated barely a quarter of an hour when my host took a violent dislike to a little slum girl who was parading across the stage bawling a sentimental song. To mark his disapproval, he stamped noisily out in the middle of the act. I was used to his whims by this time and quietly slunk out after him.

But I did not stay with his friends. I had grasped that in Dublin there was a very divided working-class movement. In the interests of our soup-kitchen I would have to try to lie down at one and the same time with both the lion and the lamb. Neutral ground was what I must find. So I followed one of our miners' brass bands home to its lodgings and asked if there was room for me.

They were living in a broken-down hotel with a lot of glittery decoration around the door; and an army of flies struggling to capture every bite of food that was put on the table. Yes, there was room for me. I was pretty tired and dropped asleep as soon as my head touched the pillow. But soon afterwards I woke, wondering if I had caught scarlet fever. My skin was itching from top to toe. I scratched sleepily. It got rapidly worse. I was obliged to get up, fumble towards the gas-jet and turn on the light.

The bed was a moving mass of fleas. I was convulsed with horror. I stripped and stood on a chair out of their reach. I wanted to fly to a bath but did not know where to go, or if there was such a thing in this primitive place. As best I could I extricated myself and my clothes and fled to the bleak dining-room downstairs. The chairs, turned upside down on the tables waiting for the morning cleaners, looked unfriendly enough; but these things are all a matter of relativity.

In just over a week I was home again with £100 to hand over to the Cowdenbeath soup-kitchen committee and promises of more to come. The promises were not kept, but as (apart from the postal workers' donation) I had been collecting penny by penny from bitterly poor people, we felt that Ireland had done reasonably well for us.

My father's position in the first weeks of the 1926 lock-out was a complicated one. He was a fireman. Firemen are known in some parts of the coalfields as deputies, in others as inspectors. As children we had listened enthralled to his stories of the time when firemen were given their name because they went into the pit ahead of the rest of the men, wrapped in wet blankets and carrying a naked light. The light tested the air for gas. If there was an excess accumulation, it was just too bad for the firemen!

In modern mining the official duty of the fireman is still to warn the men if a dangerous percentage of gas is present and to see that ventilation and other safety measures are properly attended to. The relations between firemen and other workers ought to be close and cordial. But it is usually exactly the reverse. Coal companies favour "yes" men as firemen. Men who can be bullied into scamping safety work and concentrating instead on speeding-up output.

In some coalfields, notably South Wales, the miners have so despaired of receiving loyal co-operation from the firemen that they exclude them from the miners' union. In Scotland, firemen, if willing to accept the obligations of union membership, are welcomed into the general ranks.

The test of the fireman, as of every other mine worker, comes when strike notices are served. Will he stand with the men or blackleg for the coal company?

Trade union loyalty was not something apart in our family. It was our very life. There could be no question of my father's attitude towards the stoppage. But he himself was expected to go on working. The Miners' Federation of Great Britain instructed him to do so. The pits had to be kept free from flooding and from dangerous accumulations of gas. The argument of the union was that unless this was done there would be needless danger and delay once the lock-out ended and the men (presumably victorious) were ready to resume their work. No coal must be produced but safety work must go on.

That may sound reasonable. But coal companies are never reasonable. In our district they took advantage of the presence of safety men underground to attempt to bring coal to the surface. A trickle of blackleg labour began to return to the pits. No one underground was mad enough to ask my father to handle coal. But it served the purpose of the coal company equally well if a few safety men of honourable name and reputation could be kept underground. These they hoped to use as a cover for blacklegs.

One evening in June an unofficial conference took place around our fireside between my father and two other firemen from the same pit. What were they to do? Blacklegs were being allowed to work in their pit. If they continued acting as safety men, they would be keeping the pits safe for the blacklegs. On the other hand, if they left their jobs, they would be acting contrary to trade union decisions. I watched their serious faces. One was a man of sixty. If he left the pits now, he feared he would never be given work again. The other was a middle-aged man with a large family of young children. They had not the clear black-and-white position of the miner working at the coal face. All three were socialists and loyal trade unionists. If the union had ordered them to stop work, they would have been relieved, even happy, to do so. In the end, they decided that safety workers or no safety workers, they could not stomach being in the same pit with blacklegs. They hoped too that their action would call attention to what was happening underground and help to put an end to the black-legging.

One consequence of this decision was that when the lock-out ended, the colliery where my father had worked had no further use for him. After the stoppage there was supposed to be no victimization. Men were to return to their old jobs. But coal companies never keep their word to colliers unless their employees are strongly enough organized to compel them to do so. Why should coal companies be more scrupulous than governments? In 1919 Bob Smillie was used by the Government to break the resistance of the miners. He did not know he was being so used. For Smillie was a great and honourable man. When he made a promise he meant it and stuck by it. Therefore, when Bonar Law sent him a signed letter from 11 Downing Street, promising that the recommendations of the Sankey Commission would be kept in the spirit and the letter, he believed a great advance for the miners was as good as won.

The Government knew differently. Their pledge had been merely a manœuvre to divide and disarm the miners until the coal companies and the Government were in a stronger position to fight them.

The same sort of warlike ruthlessness was now practised by the coal companies. They re-employed or blacklisted men entirely as they thought fit. A man blacklisted at his own pit had no chance of being engaged elsewhere. His bad reputation preceded him wherever he went.

The lock-out lasted from May until December. Four months after the general resumption of work my father was still idle. Each week he appeared at the colliery office asking if there was a job for him. Each week he got the same reply. The manager told him without any subterfuge about it, that he wanted "safe" men as safety men. My father replied, as you

91

may well imagine. Then, at last, he was sent for. But he was not reinstated as a fireman. He was told off to do casual labour.

After being idle so long, pit work would have been trying even to a muscular navvy. To a man of my father's delicate physique it was crucifixion.

We watched him each day trailing his limbs homeward at the end of the shift. Our mother was more than usually careful to see that hot water was ready for him to wash and that a light milk-pudding with the white of an egg whisked on top was waiting to tempt him to eat. He could not digest anything more solid until later in the evening after he had rested. And, even then, he ate very little.

No word of complaint was ever spoken and no word of sympathy ever offered. To have done either would have been a violation of my parents' ways. But I could see our mother's eyes follow his every move, ready to anticipate his slightest wish, and she, like me, knew that he was not able to walk upstairs to bed. He had to hold on by the banisters and drag himself up step by step.

We had fought and we had been beaten. The coal companies now had the whip hand. They were driving home the lessons of defeat.

All over the country men were victimized. The unions in most districts were too enfeebled by the long struggle to be able to protect them. Then there was the wonderful alibi—unemployment. Oh no, there was no such thing as victimization. It was simply that trade was bad and there was not enough work to go round.

Under cover of that kind of talk—where the unions were weak the coal companies did not even trouble to disguise what they were doing—the fight to break the spirit of a proud people went savagely on. Some miners who were active during the stoppage became permanently unemployed. Others were re-engaged then, once underground, subjected to every conceivable hardship and humiliation.

Still others were driven into exile. Told quite plainly that they were not wanted, they felt there was nothing else for it but to sell their bits of furniture and migrate, usually to the dominions. There were some sad partings. We were loath to see them go. Some of our closest relatives and friends joined the outward trek. Not Jews persecuted by Hitler's Germany. One hundred per cent Aryan British colliers driven into exile by one hundred per cent Aryan British coal-owners. And all because they thought miners should be paid more than starvation wages and had had the courage to say so. You can find such family records in every colliery village in the British Isles. Poverty, atrocious working conditions, intimidation, victimization, exile; yet there was no such thing, I was told, as a class-war. All the polite people said that to talk of such a thing was ignorant hysterics. All the popular papers and famous preachers denied its existence. Then what, in God's name, I wanted to know, were they doing to our people? I wanted an answer to that. I wanted to get to the bottom of this thing more than I wanted anything on earth.

CHAPTER VI

IN 1927 my father was blacklisted from the pits. My one brother was hoboing across Australia. I was earning my living as a schoolteacher. My income kept the family going. Most of our neighbours, from one cause or another, were worse off than we were. Many of them much worse off. There was nothing unique about what was happening to us. If there had been, these things would not be worth recording. Ours was the ordinary history of the times and place we were living in. Our circumstances were similar to thousands of other families around us. Unemployed fathers, brothers shipped off to the dominions like so many surplus head of cattle; what was there out of the ordinary in that? Nothing at all. Every other house in our street had some member unemployed and, as likely as not, other members in Canada or Australia. But that did not make it any easier for each of us. We missed my brother. The house was sadly quiet in the evening. There was not even the beating of the pit engine to break the silence as there had been when we were children.

The mining industry was progressing, so they said! The ventilation fans at the pits worked silently now!

Everything seemed strangely silent. In 1926 we had shouted and protested, we had had our meetings and our marches. In 1927 we had time to notice how shabby and disheartened everyone looked. Essential food and clothing got on credit during the lock-out had now to be paid for. So had arrears in rent; bit by bit, week by week, in instalments that left everyone bare to the bone.

The year 1927 was the one when charity organizations made it fashionable to collect old clothes and send them to the miners. Old clothes! The very idea made me fighting mad.

I was teaching in a school about two miles from my home. One day in December I suspected by the grey-blue complexion of one of the girls that she was particularly poorly clad. I say "suspected" for she was wearing a pinafore as top garment with a torn jersey showing through. I set the other children to work and took her along to the staff-room. There, in front of the fire, I found she had only a thin cotton rag of a vest under the jersey and, below the waist, no knickers or anything else. Her thin young limbs were naked to the December weather.

That was an extreme case. But almost everyone, children and adults alike, looked shabby and drab. The faces of the older people were listless and grey. There was no money for even the simplest repairs and replacements. Women sat at home patching and darning and counting over and over their few shillings, planning and scheming to see how they could make them go just a little further. Sometimes losing heart altogether. You could tell from the children in school, from their carefully washed and mended clothes and from their general demeanour, those whose mothers were still putting up a fight. It was miraculous how many still were. There were the others, of course, who had simply given in.

Our school building was in keeping with the rest of the place. It looked more like a prison than a place for children. The walls of my classroom were colour-washed in a bilious shade of pea-green. A coal-tip blotted out the view from the window. Huddled together in this cell, were forty to fifty children. They were restless, nervous and not inclined to settle down quietly. It was my job to keep them interested and orderly. Every morning at nine o'clock we valiantly began the day. The first hour went quite well. But, before the end of the afternoon, I was hanging on for dear life in a losing struggle to maintain some semblance of order.

I had no bent for this kind of teaching. I was too impatient; too much at war with my whole environment. I did not believe in what I was doing. I did not believe that there was any good reason why either the children or myself should come to terms with life as we found it in that bleak mining village.

Most of the misery I saw around me in school, in the streets and in private homes had its roots in the poverty of the place. I did not see how, within the four walls of a classroom, I could ever hope to change any of that.

96

The world seemed to me full of excellent craftsmen. People who spent themselves in teaching, in mining, in ploughing, in making bricks, in making furniture, as well as any one of these jobs could be done. It was not this individual work that was at fault. It was the general social design. The bone structure of society shows through in colliery districts with appalling obviousness. All the old moral injunctions about being honest and hard-working, thrifty and civil and you will prosper just have no relevance. You can be all those things and still starve. Fancy telling a collier to work harder! Or that he can grow rich by being thrifty. Of course, if he is ambitious and industrious he may go to night school and begin to study for a mine manager's certificate. Yes, he may do that. But, although a student in the evening he is still presumably earning his living as an ordinary collier during the day. Then the occasion comes when strike notices are served.

Some workmate has been wrongfully dismissed—or perhaps the company are attempting to dock wages already woefully low—or maybe the men are insisting on some slight improvement in their working conditions. What happens then to the young collier and his ambitions? Coalpits make no provision for any sort of no-man's-land of blurred, comfortable compromise. It has to be one thing or the other. Will he stand in with his workmates or scab for the company? That may be a bitter moment for a studious young fellow, one of real anguish and full knowledge of all that is involved. I have known young colliers, scholarly and imaginative for whom it has been all that and more. But these are the exceptions.

Much more usual, hot young blood is the first to cry out against injustice done, and there is no struggle at all. Right is right, wrong is wrong. Besides, a strike is a holiday in the open air, and mother at home will manage, somehow, as she has had to do so often before. And so the pattern is set.

It was in 1927 that with a sudden shock of recognition I realized that the woman approaching me on the main street of the town was one of my old playmates of secondary-school days. In 1917 she had been a pretty intelligent spirited girl. Now she had a baby in her arms, another clinging to her skirt and a slightly older child walking by her side. Ill-health, lack of proper food, hopeless poverty were written all over her. Later I saw where she lived. A wretched insanitary but and ben with hardly a stick of furniture in it. She had not been brought up like that any more than I had. But she had fallen in love with a young miner, married him and children had begun to arrive just when the slump years came catapulting down on our defence-less villages. He was unemployed most of the time and when working, earned almost as little as when on the dole. We, in these days, flared up if any outsider used the word "dole" and were quick to retort unemploy-ment insurance if you please, and remember we pay for it; but among ourselves we tolerated the word as a kind of shorthand.

98

The evening my old schoolmate came to supper with me we talked of local politics and of this and that and mother chimed in in a friendly, cheerful way. But when I had said good-evening to our visitor, closed the front door and returned to the living-room I found her crumpled up in front of the hearth having a good cry. The contrast between the pretty rather spoiled school-girl I had brought home ten years ago and the ill, anæmic, overburdened woman who had just left was more than her tender heart could bear. In the un-written laws that govern family relationships I had the status of eldest son rather than a daughter. I was the opinionated, self-reliant one. It was not for me to sit down beside her and weep. I made an excuse for going out and wandered wrathfully around the town. This colliery world I had returned to after four and a half student years in Edinburgh seemed grimly different from my earlier memories of it. That was partly, of course, an illusion caused by our mother's gift for putting the best face on things. Because of her a great deal of the sorrow and the squalor of the district had been veiled from us as children. I really believe that if you set her down in the middle of the Sahara with only a bucket of water and an umbrella to help her she would somehow contrive to make a home out of it.

Also between 1914 and 1921–26 (the decline began sooner in some areas than in others) the coalfields of Great Britain had caught glimpses of less savage living than ever before or since. Glimpses, that was all. The

most monstrous lies are told about the earnings of
miners during the last war. An occasional contractor
made a fancy income. The average worker earned
roughly twice as much as in pre-war days. But as prices
had also more than doubled the margin of improvement was nothing like as great as it was afterwards
made out to be. Our father, who was a skilled crafts-
man, averaged a pound a day while wages were at their
peak point. Keeping in mind wartime prices that was
by no means a princely salary.

My mother's finances have always been a mystery
to me. At long intervals when she took it into her head
to dot down exactly every penny she spent they
became a mystery to her too. She would sit on the
fender-stool in front of the fire with a note-book and
pencil on her knee and a look of consternation on her
face while my brother and I, if she had been rash
enough to tell us what she was about, would dance
around bubbling over with delight. We knew what to
expect. She would count and recount, add, subtract,
begin all over again and then again and end up by
throwing the paper angrily into the fire. On paper, she
never once was able to reduce her expenditure to her
income. We thought that very funny. But in practice
she managed miraculously. If there had been a dozen
of us instead of two, as she was fond of repeating, we
would not have had anything like so comfortable a
life.

Anyhow, for those various reasons of time and family
circumstances, my brother and I during our growing

years, were saved a good deal that the miners' children I taught during 1927 and 1928 were exposed to. We were fed on a diet consisting mainly of starch that would shock the modern dietician, but it tasted fine and was ample. Our boots were the best quality the Co-op could supply. Our Sunday coats were made of the best Galashiels tweed. Mother, a bit aghast at the price, would defend herself against an invisible assailant with her famous maxim about it never paying to buy shoddy; that the best was always the cheapest in the long run. Incidentally, she was not such a stickler about quality when it came to her own shoes and clothes. Even in medicines a distinction was made in our favour. We got sweet cascara, our parents the bitter stuff. It never occurred to us that the reason was that the bitter stuff was cheaper. Indeed, father gloried so much in retailing without slurring the minutest detail how grandmother had brewed senna tea for him when he was a boy and the other horrible concoctions he was made to swallow, that we may even have supposed they liked it that way.

Then high-water-mark of prosperity had been our Saturday evenings. There always seemed to be a shilling or two available to flood the house with a small quantity of fruit, a bag of cheap sweets and luxury beyond all, our penny fairy-tale and two comic-cuts. What else in the world was left for anyone to want? Nothing, so far as we were concerned. Unless, and that too we got, an occasional jaunt to Dunfermline to see Grandmother and Grandfather Lee and to watch the squirrels in Pittencrief Glen crack and eat the nuts we threw to them.

On one occasion, how we had the courage I don't know, we decided to do what all stylish people did when they visited the Glen. The band was playing and the open-air restaurant beside the bandstand was thronged with chattering worldly people. My small brother and I were due to leave all this gaiety and go off to have tea with our grandparents.

I decided that instead we would walk right up to a table, sit down and be served by a waitress. We had fourpence each in our pockets which seemed enough to pay for at least one cup of tea and one cake. It was the glory we were after more than the food. We knew that in the mere matter of eating we could have all we wanted later at home.

After stalking round and round the tea-rooms at least five times we screwed up enough courage to approach. Then the embarrassment and the misery of it! There was no table vacant and we had to keep walking in and out of a maze of tables with eyes staring at us, or so we imagined, from every direction. At last two people got up and we guiltily grabbed their places. Now it was all glory again. A queenly but motherly waitress came and stood over us, seeming to shield us from a world that had suddenly become rather too much for us. Somehow she knew we had only fourpence each—I forget how we got through that part of the business— but she loaded the table with currant bread and sand- wiches and cakes, and every little while she would dart

102

back to where we were sitting and whisper "eat your fill now; eat your fill". Bless her and bless her again.

But as we grew older unpleasant changes occurred. The sense of well-being that pervaded our childhood became exceedingly brittle. By the time we reached the secondary-school age, our wants had become expensive. It was no longer possible for our parents to buy us contentment for a few pence. Some class-mates had bicycles. Please could we have bicycles? Some class-mates had joined the local tennis club. Please could we have money to join the club and money to buy a racket and tennis-balls? Next it was golf or dancing lessons or a special outfit for gymnastics. In short, whatever we saw anyone else having we came home and clamoured for. Unhappily for us at the very time when our wants were mounting the family income was declining. Everything seemed to be declining. Partly, of course, we were beginning to look at the world more critically and with wider standards of comparison. But in addition there was a very real scaling down all round. We had moved from a four-roomed house to a three-roomed one. We hated that. It meant too much furniture cluttering up every corner and a much smaller living-room. But the heart of our discontents was that we were suffering from a kind of rash that breaks out sooner or later on most children from working-class homes who are sent to secondary schools. That is, we had become bitten with small-town snobbery. While this phase lasted we made life for our mother one long punishment. The family income was incongruously inadequate to meet even a quarter of our demands. Our mother peered at us anxiously over her spectacles and scraped and scrambled to meet us as far as she could. One day she came in beaming, carrying the much-coveted tennis-racket and an elegant net-bag holding six tennis-balls. The racket was presented to me. My brother borrowed it and in his enthusiasm straight away smashed it. The family fortunes never again enabled us to replace it so that was the end of our tennis careers.

About this same time an itch took possession of us to change round all the furniture in the house. We wanted to make it look smarter. The kitchen dresser was an obvious target. The shelves of the dresser were laden with useless ornaments climaxing in the inevitable "China dogs". I announced that I really must have these shelves for books. Mother was devoted to her miscellaneous crockery. Every week it was lovingly taken down, dusted or washed, and put carefully back in its place again. That week, reluctant but anxious to meet us as always, the china dogs, the remains of her wedding tea-service, weird shepherdesses, pink angels poised on sea-shells and all the other bric-a-brac, were taken down and not put back. I had won. Books, chiefly my father's and of not the slightest use to me for school purposes, arrogantly lined the dresser shelves. The household gods they had deposed were laid to rest in a large clothes-basket thrust out of sight under the bed. Next we turned our marauding eyes towards our father. He was no longer hero and superman.

104

Why, if he had anything to him, did he remain a simple colliery fireman? Why did he not make more money? We measured him against the fathers of some of our friends who were richer than we were and decided he had more brains than they had. That just increased our exasperation. Why, why, did he not use any gifts he had to make more money so that we could become small-town swells? We had no patience with him and his socialist theories and the poverty we were condemned to by his obstinacy. Money, make money, lots of it, that was what counted.

With me this silly season lasted less than a year. My brother was smitten rather more severely. One day he helped to cure me by adding to our usual impossible demands on our mother a tone of bullying and contempt that was something new. I found myself flying to her defence, mad with rage. Henceforth I stood guard over her, waiting to tomahawk the boy if he should again forget himself. Not that she took his lapse as stormily as I did. Whatever we did she had a happy knack of finding a reason for or at least a good excuse. We were tired, overstrung, working too hard at school, just thoughtless.

Soon after I had recovered from this phase, I noticed something on coming in from school one day that stabbed me to the heart. The shelves above the kitchen dresser presented a droll sight. Two tiny clearances had been made in the midst of the books and a pink angel had been timidly inserted in each. Mother must have been under the bed looking at her china and had been tempted to reinstate these two pieces. In the quick-changing, adolescent moods that young people go through, I for the moment no longer wanted to have everything my own way. "Let's put all the dishes back," I volunteered. "I think they look much nicer than books." She knew I was lying and although bewildered as to the reason, sensed that I genuinely detested those pink angels on their fatuous sea-shells. As quick as quick, she turned down the proposal and stoutly insisted that she thought the books looked much nicer than dishes and she would rather that they were kept where they were. I knew she was lying just as she knew I was lying, but there the matter ended. The books remained on the shelves and the next day even the pink angels were again slumbering in the basket beneath the bed.

By 1921 there was no longer any doubt that the post-war slump had marked the colliery districts down for heavy punishment. The coal strike of that year meant that everyone had to exhaust any small savings that might have been assembled when wages were higher. And the following year I had somehow to be financed to begin life as a University student. How that was done I have already described.

But in 1927, looking back on even our worst times, we seemed to have been living in a golden Eldorado compared with what was now happening. The year 1927 was like living in a beleaguered city. You felt that relief must come soon or you die. If anyone had tried to say that more than a decade of this grey death in life lay ahead, we would have laughed unbelievingly. "There will be bloody revolution sooner than that," the average collier and his family would have told you. And meant it, too! 1927 was a year of bitter political controversy and recrimination. Almost every evening we held meetings. These were mostly stormy, acrimonious affairs in keeping with the temper of the times. After the fiascos of 1919, 1921 and 1926, the Communist Party had a rich arsenal of material with which to attack the Labour Party.

According to the gospel as preached by the spate of Communist orators who were let loose during those years in the advanced industrial areas, all Labour leaders were traitors, fakirs, twisters and parasites sucking the blood of the poor. I detested the harsh, mechanical vocabulary and the insensitive indiscriminate abuse that characterized Communist Party utterances. And I resented bitterly the virulence of the attack made on those of us inside the Labour Party who were doing our utmost to destroy the right-wing MacDonald, Thomas, Henderson influences.

One day in Cowdenbeath High Street I listened to a young Communist orator declaiming in the usual fashion. Some hours later I passed him in the street and on a sudden impulse went up and demanded he should come home with me. I was determined to have this thing out. I wanted to know whether a goodly portion of the abuse he had been scattering around him was grounded in ignorance or deliberate malice. Did he really believe that the MacDonalds, Thomases,

107

Hendersons and the rest were as deep-dyed villains as he had made them out to be? And more particularly, did he seriously contend that families like my own representing the left-wing point of view inside the official movement were actuated by anything other than a burning desire to end poverty and establish socialism?

By the end of the evening I had dropped my hectoring tone. My friend, the enemy, took the wind out of my sails by a very simple line of argument. The trouble with good little idealists like me, he retorted, was that we were for ever concerned with motives, intentions, subjective states of mind. That was territory better left to the psychologist. As for himself, as a Marxist, scientific socialist, he was not interested in what went on inside the heads of Ramsay MacDonalds and James Maxtons and Jennie Lees. He was solely concerned with the objective results of their political behaviour. Looked at objectively, was I prepared to defend leaders who had thrown away the revolutionary opportunities of the immediate post-war years, who had given us Black Friday in 1921, the disastrously ill-planned General Strike of 1926 and who showed every symptom of going on to further fiascos and betrayals unless they could be ruthlessly got rid of?

I jumped in impatiently at this point saying he could cut out all that line of talk. The issue between us was something quite different. I no more supported the right-wing leadership of the Labour Party than he did. Only, by working inside instead of outside the party, I was making my opposition a hundred times more effective than his could ever be. Also, he had better remember that the Labour Movement was something much bigger than a handful of leaders. There were devoted, disinterested men and women campaigning for socialism in every corner of Great Britain and managing to do so without sickening the general public and degrading themselves by descending to filthy, slanderous attacks on individuals every time they opened their mouths.

"Quite true, quite true, Comrade," he came back sarcastically. "The Communist Party is kept outside the Labour Party, but the I.L.P. is allowed to remain inside. The I.L.P. is the darling of the Labour Party. For how could the Jimmy Thomases and the Ernest Bevins and the Hendersons get away with it if they had not the James Maxtons to whitewash them in the eyes of the ordinary worker? Nice, kind, sentimental, witty speeches from Maxton that slide down as easily as an ice-cream wafer and make everyone feel what a happy family the Labour Party is at bottom. I tell you, Comrade Lee, your kind are the worst of the lot. Romantic revolutionaries like you have got to be discredited. You are a drug blinding the masses. Without you the right-wing gang would be seen and exposed in their true light. Without you they could not survive a single day. And so you see, Comrade Lee, I shall go on denouncing you and your slavering, sentimental I.L.P." At this point, mother, with an overcoat thrown over her nightdress, put her head anxiously round the

109

kitchen door and asked if I knew it was two o'clock in the morning and that the alarm-clock would be ringing for father to go off to work in less than three hours and that we were making such a din, no one could get a wink of sleep.

Hastily, we said good-night and shook hands and agreed to meet and finish the argument another night.

I went to bed and lay awake for some time with two words jumping and tumbling around me—objective, subjective, objective, subjective, subjective, objective. Was it true that socialists like myself were merely giving a false front to the Labour Party behind which leaders I neither trusted nor respected could the more easily mislead and betray?

The following week there was a much advertised Communist Party propaganda meeting in the town and I went along to it determined to be "objective". After three hours of communist oratory I crept home feeling dirtied and dejected. Whatever I was looking for, this certainly was not it. I hated the nauseating reiteration of the words traitors, fakirs, applied indiscriminately to all and sundry; I was impatient with the cheap quackery of infallibility that all Communist Party spokesmen laid claim to. I found nothing warming, sustaining in this diet of hate and mechanical Marxist clichés. This was at best a barren caricature of what I believed a revolutionary socialist party should be. I turned back with a feeling of going home to the broad Labour Movement. There, quite plainly, was where I belonged. There were fewer people claiming

infallibility in its ranks, there was room for a vigorous
exchange of views, there was the hope of turning
this vast powerful organization that three generations
of my family had loved and laboured for, away from
the damning influences of MacDonaldism and forward
to socialism.

My natural bent, although I hated it when anyone
else said so, was evangelical. MacDonald himself was
not much better at painting the sorrows of the poor,
the beauty and dignity of the Promised Land of
socialism—and of trusting to Providence somehow to
jump the gap between the distressful present and that
beatific future.

I had endless opportunities for exercising my talents.
Every week-end, sometimes week nights as well, I was
off on a round of socialist propaganda meetings. At
first it was hard going. I would carefully prepare and
write out a speech with a beginning, a middle and an
end. Once on the platform I forgot most of what I had
written. I was no use at reciting from memory or
reading aloud from a manuscript. My temperament
made speaking a hit or a miss affair. I had to know
beforehand what I wanted to say, then trust to the
inspiration of the moment for the right words and
imagery in which to say it.

I had, or imagined I had, when first I began to
attempt to speak in public, one grave handicap, and, also,
an advantage I was not entitled to have. A great, husky
collier in the Lothians (most miners are small) made me
conscious of the first; my grandfather of the second.

I had been booked to speak at a meeting in one of the mining villages near Edinburgh. That was back in 1924. The local secretary wrote that he would meet me when I arrived and take me to the hall.

On arrival, I jumped off the train and looked around hopefully for my escort. The platform gradually emptied until I was sure that one particular man who was scrutinizing all the passengers must be looking for me. I went up to him and announced myself. He looked down at me and said just these two words, "Great God!" But they were eloquently spoken. I was nineteen. My round, red face and snub nose made me look even younger than I was. He was plainly filled with panic. Had he chalked the streets and booked a hall and made all arrangements for a really important propaganda meeting with only this to see him through the evening?

I trailed miserably along by his side, now in a bigger panic than he was. I was trying to repeat to myself the speech that I had so carefully prepared. But my mind was a complete blank. We reached the hall. It was packed and impatient. I was rushed through the central passage, thrown on to the platform, introduced in thirty seconds and left to it. Somehow I staggered through. When I sat down I had not the faintest idea of what I had said. I wanted only to escape. Yet no one had laughed at me. That was the incredible thing. No one had laughed! They had sat quite still. At the end they even applauded.

That was in 1924. For several years that "Great

God" rang in my ears. The effect it had on me was that always when I had platform work to do I did everything I could to make myself look older.

One spring day in 1927 Grandfather Lee paid one of his rare visits to Lochgelly. We went often enough to Dunfermline to visit him, but it was not often he found time to come to us. That happened only when there was something special afoot. I arrived in from school just after four o'clock. Tea had already begun. The table had been drawn over to the fire so that he could sit in the most comfortable arm-chair.

As I came in, he got up from his chair and came over to meet me. We shook hands which for an undemonstrative family like ours was in itself unusual. Then he said, very proudly, "Master of Arts, Bachelor of Laws". I had just completed my LL.B. degree. I had not taken the work seriously. For me it had meant six months' cramming after I finished the M.A. degree and thus earning the second half of the £100 law scholarship that I had won the year before. The condition attached to the payment of the second instalment of £50 was that the holder must complete the degree examinations.

I was pleased that he should be so pleased and, at the same time, felt what a fraud it all was. The universities were turning out ten-a-penny graduates in large droves several times a year. Most of us remained largely illiterate. For some months before examinations, we crammed to the teeth. A month or two afterwards, we had forgotten all we had learned.

All that remained was our certificates, and in the case of those who were particularly obtuse, a feeling of superiority over people who had not been initiated into these mystic rites.

But often at my meetings I saw the faces of elderly and middle-aged colliers looking up towards me from the body of the hall, reconciled to my youth because of the letters after my name. It is part of Scotch working-class pride to deny any respect for University degrees, but part of its practice, particularly inside the Labour Movement, to pay far too much deference to them.

I knew how my grandfather's, even my father's, generation felt about education. They were very romantic about it. They thought of it as a kind of lamp to light the feet of their children, so that we need not stumble and hurt ourselves as they had done; or as armour buckled around us so that we could meet in fair fight all who stood in our way. They never doubted that our fight would be anything other than their fight and with them and of them and for them.

Through long, difficult years, men who felt limited by their own lack of formal education, fought that we should not be so handicapped. That fight was all part of the struggle to build a self-confident working-class. Jude the Obscure, fearful of his own limitations and impressed by the training of his superiors, vowed that his children should be numbered among the Initiated. But the pity of it is that only one in a thousand of those who have benefited from his efforts have any idea of their immediate social and political antecedents.

In a very direct sense those of us who are graduates from the industrial parts of Great Britain are the children of the Labour Movement. Our education has been wholly or partly paid for by the public authorities. On those public bodies it is always the socialist members (with an occasional Liberal) who press for free schools, free books, access to secondary schools and maintenance grants to help us through training-college or university.

It is very hard on the old idealistic socialist when he sees graduates from working-class homes turn into small-town snobs. He had counted on them to be his invaluable allies. He cannot understand what has gone wrong, for he seldom realizes the limitations of the educational processes they have been through.

I do not remember either in elementary or secondary school a single history lesson in which I was given the slightest idea of the life of ordinary working-people, still less of their distinctive organizations.

At home, from my father's books, I read a great deal about the year 1848. I read about the potato famine in Ireland, of the Chartist agitations all over Britain, of starving children sent to gaol for stealing food, of miners working for two and sixpence a day, of boat-loads of helpless Irish labourers dumped in the Lanark-shire coalfields to prevent any successful agitation for an improvement in wages—and much of a similar kind.

At school, believing it to be history, I was taught a

great number of fairy stories about kings and queens and warring nobles. When children read, they identify themselves with the characters they read about. I was always a king or a queen or, at least, a great feudal lord. I was never a collier stealing from hunger and punished for stealing.

I am not really complaining about how history is taught in schools. That would be a mere waste of time. I do not expect education in England, Scotland, Ireland, Russia or Germany, to be anything other than propaganda in favour of whatever happens to be the controlling power in the State. Some day the world may be run on something other than the murder and plunder principle. But until then, no one country dare allow its schools to be anything except propaganda factories. Russia is a case in point. Within its own frontiers it has overthrown the plunder principle, but the Soviet Union is conscious of enemies all round it. It does not feel safe. All teaching material is, therefore, subjected to the most rigid kind of censorship. The young Soviet citizen, like the young Britisher or German, is carefully drilled in that version of history and of current affairs that is best calculated to help forward whatever happens to be the immediate purposes of the State.

Caught up in that kind of tangle, there is only one thing that a serious socialist movement can do. It is bound to regard working-class education, quite independently of the ordinary school system, as one of its key activities. It is bound to train advocates who can teach adult audiences the history and objectives of the organized working-class movement. That is how any reputable socialist propagandist sees his job. That, at least, is how I saw mine.

That day in 1927 when my grandfather came specially to Lochgelly to show me how pleased he was, I did not start any argument. I was happy to see him and tried to show him so in every way I could. But I felt hopelessly out at elbows with most of his values and expectations. He was still at bottom a gentle, civilized nineteenth-century radical who believed that socialism would be brought about mainly by Acts of Parliament and would come in gradual, inevitable stages.

His outlook was more representative of the Labour Movement than mine was. It was not so much what he said as what he assumed. He took it for granted, for instance, that whenever the public should choose to return a majority Labour Government, large chunks of socialist legislation would be passed through the House of Commons, obstructed a little by the House of Lords, but ultimately become law and, as such, be universally respected and enforced.

Respect for the Law, for Parliament, for public opinion were to be sufficient to restrain anyone who might feel like obstructing or resorting to extra-constitutional methods.

It is remarkable how many socialists of that generation, even those whose industrial experience should have protected them against such lavish assumptions, cling to this simple faith.

117

All his life, in the disputes between colliers and coal-owners, my grandfather had been familiar with lies, double-dealing and crude victimization. Coalowners don't hesitate to bring soldiers and additional police into the mining towns to be used against the miner if they think that, by doing so, they can better gain their ends. My grandfather had seen policemen's batons used against his workmates. In 1921, then barely seventeen, I got caught in the middle of Cowdenbeath High Street in a fight between policemen and miners. I was cycling home from Dunfermline library with a bundle of books tied to the back of my bicycle. The pressure of the crowd forced me to dismount. They went surging past me, growling and cusring at the police. I had no room to turn my bicycle or I would have run too. My sense of property must have been stronger than my sense of fear! I clung to my bicycle and my books and stood my ground, dazed by the quick, backward flow of the crowd. Still bewildered, I found a line of policemen with drawn batons literally towering over me. Some of the younger miners were throwing stones at them from closes at the side of the High Street. One was beautifully aimed. I saw the blood trickling down the side of a policeman's face. Everyone was beside himself with rage. Tempers had snapped. There was a "free for all" for a few minutes then, quite suddenly, it was all over. I had to walk home the rest of the way for the frame of my bicycle had been twisted in the general mix-up. I felt pleased and excited and angry all in one. For me this was a childish adventure without any serious risk. But I did not forget it. Miners, it seemed, when they set out to improve their wages and conditions, had to reckon with the physical forces of the State as well as with the money and influence of the coalowners.

In that same 1921 strike, soldiers had been quartered at the pits. That was two years after Bob Smillie and the miners had been tricked by the Sankey Commission. Lies, batons, broken promises, soldiers' bayonets, all these we were familiar with in the coalfields. Yet, by some strange alchemy, our socialist movement still trusted, still believed in peaceful evolutionary change provided only a Labour Government sat at Westminster.

I was bothered by those inconsistencies. But not too deeply. After all there were plenty of others beside myself to do the thinking and the worrying. And, anyhow, I was too busy to have much time for thought. There was always an endless stream of meetings to be addressed.

CHAPTER VII

WHENEVER a telegram arrived in our house mother ripped it open at once and steadied her trembling eyes as well as she could to read what it had to say. Letters were private affairs and as such respected and left untouched. But a telegram was a calamity. She had better be the first to know, so that she could break the news. As I got myself more and more involved in political activities and telegrams began to arrive quite frequently, she relaxed a bit; but never quite. She never entirely lost that little tremor of fear whenever she saw the post-office message-boy jump off his bicycle in front of her gate and waited for him to call out "Telegram for you, Mrs. Lee."

One July day when I came in from school she handed me the usual pink telegram-form and I read, "Labour Movement in Shotts desires to nominate you for Parliamentary Candidature of North Lanark under I.L.P. auspices reply per return as to your considering same. Dewar Secy, 5 Benhar Rd. Shotts."

I must have looked startled or upset or something, for immediately I laid it down, mother lifted the wire and read it for the second time, then puzzled, inquired,

"It is nothing serious, is it?" She had been quite at her ease after glancing over it when it first arrived, for no one was dead; no one in trouble.

"No, no, mother, nothing serious. Just I.L.P. business." That kept her from worrying. I could settle down to the meal she had prepared for me and decide what to say in reply.

I was in a mild kind of panic. It was one thing to address propaganda meetings, to take part in local affairs, even to steady your nerves sufficiently to carry your feet to the rostrum in national party conferences when there was some issue before party members about which you were so violently agitated that you felt you must speak or bust.

But a Parliamentary candidature? And in a constituency where the sitting Tory Member had a majority of only 2,028. That meant that when the election came our people ought to win. Ought to. But supposing I was candidate and made a hash of things. I thought of the great May Day demonstration I had addressed in Shotts less than two months before. That thought was warming. It had been an entirely working-class and mainly collier gathering. What a cold windy place that public park of theirs was! But there was nothing cold about the people themselves. Why should I be afraid of them? They were almost identical in outlook and needs to the Fife people I had grown up among. Yes, yes, after all, the telegram only asked consent to nominate me along with others to go before a selection committee. Yes, all right, it was their suggestion, not mine. They surely knew what they were about. I had no money. Every penny for the organization work of the division and the election campaign itself would have to be found by the local movement. And I was dismally young. But I smiled when I remembered that young women between twenty-one and thirty would have the vote for the first time at the next general election. The Tory Party would be bound to throw bouquets to this new section of the electorate. It could hardly at the same time attack me on account of my age!

The following February the sitting Tory Member for North Lanark died. A by-election was precipitated. I found myself elected to Parliament with a majority of 6,578.

The by-election caused great excitement throughout the constituency and more than the usual national interest. For everyone knew it was only a matter of months until a general election must take place. Socialists everywhere were delighted with the result. It confirmed the high hopes they already held that their party was soon to become the government of Great Britain.

Even in the rush and splutter of that first contact with North Lanark, I was appalled by the poverty of the place. I was at home in colliery districts. I thought I knew exactly what to expect. But this was worse than anything I had ever known. In some of the smaller villages living conditions were such that one might have been back in the time of the Chartist agitations and the hungry forties. Everywhere there was a housing famine. For years I had been repeating from public platforms the statistics of Scottish housing conditions. Half the population living in one or two-roomed houses, seventy-five per cent of the people of Lanarkshire living in one or two-roomed houses. I was now learning in all its unforgettable squalor what that Lanarkshire figure meant. Unemployment was another torment. Desperate men and women packed those 1929 meetings clamouring for work. And those in jobs were equally dissatisfied for wages and working conditions throughout the county left them little better off than the unemployed.

I dubbed the eighth hour underground of the collier's working-day "Baldwin's hour". A feature of the election was the promise that the Labour Party empowered me to make that one of the first acts of a Labour Government would be to reduce the working hours of miners from eight to seven without any corresponding reduction in wages.

After Lanark came London and initiation into the ways of the House of Commons. The Trevelyan family probably saved me from making a too ungainly entrance. I was living with them during my first few days in London. An hour or two before I was due to leave for the House, Lady Trevelyan had a sudden inspiration. Did I know exactly what I was expected to do when the Speaker called on me to take my place? In walking down the centre of the Chamber towards his chair, three times I would have to stop, keeping in

123

step with my two sponsors, and bow neatly. "Now," she said, striding to the opposite end of their long drawing-room, "imagine I am the Speaker and let me see you bow." I bent my back but made the expected mistake of keeping my head sticking into the air. That was not at all graceful. I would have to try again and this time incline my head properly. This all seemed to me rather a fantastic way of fighting the class-war, but as I was a novice sprawling around in an unfamiliar environment, I was glad enough to be saved from making any unnecessary blunders.

In the inner lobby of the House of Commons, Bob Smillie and James Maxton were waiting for me. I had chosen them as my sponsors. Maxton, leader of the I.L.P. and friend as long as I could remember. Our beloved Bob Smillie, my grandfather's mate and miners' leader and family friend even before I was born. Incidentally, this choice of sponsors was my first disagreement with Labour Party officialdom. The head office had selected Margaret Bondfield and Tom Kennedy to introduce me, but in facing Parliament for the first time I wanted to have those other two whose texture I had been familiar with all my life, within touching distance. I was a good deal more nervous than pride would allow me to show.

Not that there was any need for me to be so apprehensive. I found my colleagues in the House of Commons almost stiflingly affable. That is, with the exception of a number of the Scottish Miners' M.P.'s whose faces, for reasons that at that time I was totally unable

124

to fathom, curdled up like a bowl of sour milk whenever we accidentally collided.

The real terror of my life during this first year in London were the journalists. At that time I had no acquaintances among them and did not understand them nor the compulsions that made them act as they did. Also, before leaving Lochgelly, the first to invade my privacy had made me mistrustful of the whole lot. I was still teaching but was due to leave school and begin the North Lanark campaign at the end of the week. On the Wednesday of that week I rushed home as usual for a midday meal and found a strange-looking creature embedded in the living-room sofa. Mother had placed a small table in front of him supporting her ample bread-scone-cake conception of what makes a hospitable forenoon tea. I bristled up spying danger whenever I set eyes on him. When the "story" appeared in the press my suspicions were confirmed. My poor mother declared she was afraid to show her head outside the door. What would the neighbours think of her for telling all those lies? For what either of us had actually said had been totally ignored and a fantastic sob-story invented in its place. I was outrageously angry and decided that if that was journalism and journalists, I wanted nothing to do with either. I brought this same attitude with me to London. I simply could not understand why what I looked like, what I wore, my favourite breakfast and whether I thought whiskers should be curled upwards or downwards had anything to do with the serious political purposes that engaged my working hours. And I was most particularly determined that whatever place I made my home in London should remain inviolate. I laugh now when I think of the lengths that Annie and I went to to ensure that no press man, especially press photographer, should invade us. Annie was my charlady, six feet tall, muscular and blindingly blonde. She polished floors superbly and was in every way magnificent except that she liked to smoke and scatter tobacco ash around all the time she was at work. I was then renting 28 Dean Street, Soho, from Clifford Allen (later alas, Lord Allen of Hurtwood). Apparently one of the things about this minute top-story flat in the heart of London that had attracted him, was that Karl Marx had lived and worked there for a number of years. Actually therefore the place had a certain legitimate "news" interest. But I was totally blind to any other consideration except a stubborn determination not to be "done" a second time. Several times when an incident in the House made the I.L.P. group "news", Annie reported that these there people were knocking at the door downstairs and peering over the window, she would further report "Keep back, Miss, keep back. They got cameras." We took it as seriously as a military engagement and when the knocking had died away, celebrated the victory. Annie's real ambition was to pour a bucket of water from the top-story window on to the heads of the enemy below, but I thought that was going a bit too far. This was hardly a sophisticated approach to public life. But I had not been sent to London because I was sophisticated. I had been sent there because I vehemently resented the poverty and slums and unemployment that was sapping away the very life of the industrial population of Scotland. And had persuaded the majority of the electorate of North Lanark that these were not acts of God about which nothing could be done but man-made evils that men could also remedy.

I was not likely to forget that Scottish background. But even if I had wanted to every post brought a torrent of reminders. Oh! those mails!

Ex-soldiers of 1914–18 too ill to work but somehow not entitled to pensions; men hurt in the pits, able at most for light work but no light work available and compensation being stopped. Women living in two-roomed cottages with one of the rooms so damp that the water made rivulets down the wall and the whole family had to huddle together, sleeping and waking, day and night, when they were sick and when they were well, all in the one apartment. Old people hungry because they could not spin out their ten-shilling pension even as supplemented by a shilling or two from the Public Assistance Board to cover food and fuelling to the end of the week. Unemployed men in areas where no work was available cut off benefit for "not genuinely seeking work". Lads stranded, workless, penniless in Australia or Canada and wondering how they could get home. Other lads unemployed at home and wondering how they could get out to the fine openings that the papers talked about in the Dominions. Women in new council houses, worried and frightened out of their wits as they made the discovery that it now took more for lighting, cooking, heating and the barest repairs than they had had to budget for in their old houses and finding themselves shorter on food rations than they had ever been in their lives before. Optimists who had acquired furniture, bicycles, wireless-sets on the instalment system and could not keep up their payments. What rights had they? Could the firm carry the goods away and could they claim back any of the money they had so laboriously paid in? One evening in the House of Commons I was working away at a pile of "cases" on a side-table in one of the division lobbies. That was my dodge for getting on with correspondence and at the same time being on hand when the division bell rang. Maxton sauntered along the lobby. Looking quizzically down at me, he tapped with his long brown fingers the enormous bundle of letters I was ploughing my way through and said in his slow disarming drawl, "You had better make up your mind, you know, whether you mean to be a socialist Member of Parliament or another b—— welfare worker like Geordie"—chuckling and nodding in the direction of his bosom pal, George Buchanan M.P. Only Maxton could sum up his friends so pointedly yet without giving offence. I laughed, seeing the justice of his remark. But all the same letters had to be answered.

Twice a day I looked apprehensively at the fresh

pile of "cases" that arrived for me. It seemed as if the floodgates had opened and all the pent-up sorrow and hopes and fears that had accumulated in North Lanark since the time of the Boer War were streaming down to London. Those letters haunted me. Some months later Roden Buxton passed along that same division lobby and found me drowning in letters at that same table. He stopped and helpfully suggested that I ought to have a secretary. I told him I agreed but that a Parliamentary allowance of £400 a year that had to cover living expenses in London, family commitments in Scotland and lots of other odds and ends besides left a margin that barely paid for the postage-stamps I needed. To pay a trade-union rate of pay to a competent secretary was just out of the question. The next day he persuaded me to meet Dorothy Hawkin who, as part of her service to the Socialist movement, was apparently willing to work for me as a voluntary unpaid secretary. I was not keen. From my men colleagues I had heard a good deal about fancy people of independent means who volunteered to act as secretaries and turned out to be more trouble than they were worth. But soon afterwards, I found myself racing at a pace probably never seen before through the grey corridors of Westminster and reaching the secretaries' room, breathless and apologetic if I was so much as five minutes late. I hoped one day to arrive there first and be able to look at Dorothy in the superior way she looked at me. But it never happened that way. Always she would be there at her desk, the

.morning mail opened, read, routine letters answered and the rest waiting for me. I had a superb secretary and was very proud of her.

The actual time I had now to spend on correspondence was more than quartered. But "cases" remained the bane of my life. My difficulty was that I had no gift for thinking in abstract categories. My mind reduced everything to the personal, immediate and concrete. An old man's letter, though I may never have met him, telling me how he was trying yet failing to live on his old-age pension, was my friend, John Garrity, appealing to me. John, with the great leonine head that I had taken so much pleasure in looking at. John, who was brave and gentle, and so proud; and such good fun too with his quick Irish wit and belligerence. Year after year he attended our Lochgelly I.L.P. branch meetings with religious regularity. He was branch treasurer for a long time and although he had no other income than his old-age pension, we knew we had the safest treasurer in the country. Nearing seventy the time came when John, who all his life had been doing for other people, himself began to need looking after. He had no one to keep house for him. He had only his pension and the usual shilling or two allowed by the public assistance authority. The day came when he was no longer able to keep an independent fireside. They found him a place in a charity institution in Edinburgh. He was well enough treated there after the manner of such places. But he was not happy. He wanted to go home to Lochgelly. He wanted to be free

130

to go in and out as he pleased. He wanted to be back among the people he was used to and liked best. John is only one of thousands. If he had had even as little as a pound a week in those last few years it would have made all the difference to him between independence and cold impersonal charity; between life and death in life. A pound a week is not a fancy income. We should blush to offer old people so little. But it is twice as much as John was allowed.

It was the same with letters about men stranded in the Dominions. Always it was my brother I saw. Mostly the letters came from districts in Scotland that I knew very well; letters sent by mothers aching to know if their sons could be found work or brought home again. I knew every minutest nuance of the grief such women feel. I had cause to know. Never a day in life past that my own mother's thoughts did not go out to her son, wondering about him, always wondering. Was he well? Did he have a warm meal when he needed one? Had he a comfortable bed at night? Was he home-sick or liking the new life? Not quite eighteen was so young to be sent so far away from home. And letters took such a long time. Six weeks going and another six weeks for a reply to come back. Anything could happen in that time.

It had been the same with Grandmother Lee as it now was with my mother. Always when I went to see my grandmother she used to ask me the same question. "How old are ye noo, Jen?" "Ten, Grannie," I would say. Or as the years passed, "twelve, Grannie," "fifteen, Grannie," "seventeen", "twenty", "twenty-seven". "Twenty-seven," she would repeat (I was twenty-eight when she died), "then it's twenty-seven years come Michaelmas since Charlie gaed awa'." Charlie was her first-born. He left for Canada when I was three months old. I was my grandmother's calendar. Always from my age she told herself the unbelievable. Charlie had been gone all those years. Charlie, the quiet, corrie-handed, scholarly one. Charlie, who went out with a neighbour's lad star-gazing at night; coming home at dawn just in time to put on his pit clothes and be off to the pit. Charlie— and here pride and wrath would struggle in her voice— who saved up along with his neighbour thirty good Scotch pounds then spent it all, yes, every penny of it, on a telescope to look at the stars. What was he looking for? What did he think he would find? He was shy with strangers she would say. But mind you, Jen, never wi' you. It was a strange thing. You were just a wee babby. And he would lift you up and carry you frae room to room. My grandmother had another ten sons and daughters. You would think that in such a crowd one more or less would never have been missed. Yet all her life she thought about Charlie and kept wondering about him. For the first few years after he left he wrote regularly and sent home a pound whenever he could. Then, mysteriously, entirely out of character, letters abruptly stopped. There were rumours that he had been killed in "labour trouble" on the west coast of America, but nothing definite was ever discovered.

Just silence and grandmother left counting the years and never giving up hope.

As a child, always when I heard the Jacobite songs—"Will ye no come back again"—"Far over yon Seas"—"Bonny Charlie's Noo Awa'"—"A Wee Birdie cam' to our ha' Door", my grandmother's Charlie got mixed up with the Stuart Charlie. With her I am sure there was not even a mixing. It was her own Charlie that all the songs were for. After my brother left we waited long weeks for letters; and worried when they were delayed. If we had known definitely what was happening to him, when he had money in his pocket, when he was unemployed and "broke", it would have been less wearing than the uncertainty. Those of our neighbours who had friends abroad felt and worried just as we did. I would hear a voice shouting to mother in passing, "How is your boy getting on, Mrs. Lee? I had a letter from our John last week." Then the tongues would be busy, sharing news, finding relief in telling one another their hopes and fears, boasting joyously when the exile was prospering, sometimes confiding, sometimes hiding the worst of the truth those times when parcels and postal-orders small in themselves but a harsh cut into a working man's income were being sent off to tide the immigrant over a particularly bad patch.

In the seventeenth century there was a considerable exodus of population from Scotland and Ireland to the continent of Europe. Men without property or prospects hired themselves as mercenaries to fight the battles of other powers for a few pence per day. They came to be called the "wild geese". In the twentieth century the wild geese are still on the wing. People without property, without continuity, without a past. People who leave no trace behind, who walk on water. Wild geese blown hither and thither by circumstances over which they have so little control. Never rooted for long in any one soil. Without property and therefore with no enduring ties. Most of us need roots. But the continuity is always being broken. A few links are forged then once again the chain snaps. We must start all over again perhaps at the opposite ends of the earth.

You may want to say how morbid, how unenterprising! It is a splendid thing to be an empire-builder. To go off and conquer the world anew.

My experience is that those who talk in that way know nothing of the iron compulsions of poverty. And still less of the suffering of women who rear families only to lose them while they are still little more than children. I have heard so many women say, "If only I could see him again—just once."

Well-to-do people seldom know that kind of hurt. They can go and if their heart is breaking, they can come home again. But ours seldom come back. The awful finality of those long ocean crossings is very hard to bear. Hope never dies that your own may be exempted from the general fate but you know very well that the majority of penniless immigrants have little chance of ever again seeing their home people; as little as had murderers and thieves sentenced for life in the old days and shipped off to Botany Bay.

When civil servants and soldiers are working abroad, it is made possible for them, if they so wish, to return home from time to time. No one has ever been able to convince me that to make provision so that lads from British pits, factories and farms persuaded to emigrate by propaganda, mostly Government-controlled or inspired, that is at best a misleading tissue of half-truths, should even once in all their after-life be given a similar privilege would impose a strain upon the resources of the British Empire greater than it could bear. But in 1929 I had already learned this curious fact about national expenditure. A Conservative minister of the Crown can look you in the eye and quite solemnly assure you that to add even one shilling a week to the old-age pension is a financial impossibility. To do so would overburden industry; kill the goose that laid the golden egg. The old people would be the first to suffer. Such an effort to help them, however well intentioned (and of course your heart was never in question; it was your head only that was at fault) would produce disastrous results and might make it impossible to continue even their present allowances. You can switch round from pensions to the care of sick people, or children, or work schemes or housing and always the same formula is applied. The Government is already doing the maximum that the economics of the situation allow.

When first I sat in Parliament and heard Conservative Ministers talk like that I listened half antagonized, half admiring. It was obviously second nature for them to look at the world in that way. Super-tax payers and paupers existing side by side in no way discountenanced them. The earth and all its fruits belonged to a small group of the elect. Theirs the pits and shipyards and factories. Apparently they even thought it right that they should gobble up mountains and forests and great heather-clad commons. And their friends in Parliament could be relied on to defend every iota of their monopolies. The many, the ordinary people might be suffered to exist so long as they kept to the main highways and to the special compounds built to accommodate them—and tolerated even there only on condition of paying fabulous ground rent and other tribute.

It was too obvious to be worth saying that if the same Ministers of the Crown had had to find an additional hundred million or even a thousand million to pay for extra soldiers to police property, they would have been able to find the money. It was simply a question of what was thought to be important and urgent.

I prayed to my own particular gods that whenever working people should come to power they would have this same sublime sustaining sense of what was due to them. That they in turn would allow nothing to stand in their way.

CHAPTER VIII

MR. STANLEY BALDWIN was British Prime Minister in 1926. That was the year of the General Strike. The year when the coalowners of Great Britain were able to call to their assistance, in their fight against colliers, the entire powers of the State, not excluding its soldiers and police. The year when the working people of Great Britain were taught that effective resistance to wage-cuts is a revolutionary act.

Mr. Stanley Baldwin won handsomely in 1926. The General Strike collapsed; the miners were starved into submission; the Trade Disputes Act was amended in a way that the Government hoped would permanently cripple the unions.

And the aftermath of all that was the defeat of Mr. Baldwin and his Government in the general election of 1929.

There was great excitement everywhere when it was found that a second Labour Government had been elected. Working people felt that they had scored a sensational victory. This was their answer to 1926. But the excitement did not last long. It was soon followed by bewilderment, disappointment and a good deal of despair. The external events of that time are well known. The year 1931 was one of exceptional economic depression all over the world. Labour leaders found they had to abandon most of their election promises. Wages, pensions, housing, education, yes, it was desirable to spend a great deal more money on all of these. But Mr. Philip Snowden, as Chancellor of the Exchequer, could not find the money. He consulted the directors of the Bank of England and the leaders of the Federation of British Industries. Very sorry, Mr. Snowden, he was told, we cannot find money for your socialist programme, and if you try to press your policy through Parliament in spite of us, you will make nothing of it. You will simply precipitate economic chaos and collapse. Indeed we go further than that. You must go back to your party and tell it that wages must be reduced, social services restricted, unemployment benefits cut. And if it does not agree, then the first effect of its obstinacy will be the unparalleled disaster and disgrace of England going off the gold standard.

No one seemed to know what going off the gold standard exactly would mean. But the very vagueness of the threat made it all the more effective. Mr. MacDonald lost his head entirely. At the height of the crisis he rose to speak in the House of Commons, brandishing a German note of the early post-war inflationary period. If we went off the gold standard, our money would soon become worthless. Mr. Snowden apparently agreed with him. The bulk of the Labour

138

Party sulked. They did not know what to make of it all. But there was one thing that they stuck on. "If the situation was as desperate as it was made out to be, then let those who could best afford to, make the main sacrifices. Above all, don't ask the unemployed, already far below subsistence level, to accept a further ten per cent reduction." The next step was the formation of a National Government, the country going off the gold standard, instead of the predicted collapse, quite a revival in export trade, everyone beginning to breathe more freely again, and the Labour opposition coming out of its corner and boldly declaring, "Bah! we knew all the time it was only a bit of spooking. The crisis was never half so serious as it was made out to be. This was the Tory Party up to its usual tricks: frightening the electorate with highly-coloured scare stories. And Mac-Donald is a traitor for having lent himself to their infamous scheming."

The main brunt of Labour's attack fell on Mac-Donald. Its favourite explanation for the whole miserable fiasco of Labour's period in office was, "It was all due to MacDonald's vanity and love of a Lord".

Maybe, but that does not account for Philip Snowden. There was no love lost between these two men. Yet, for his own quite separate and sufficient reasons, Labour's Chancellor of the Exchequer also crossed to the ranks of the Tories. The spiritual biography of Philip Snowden is a conventional one; youthful idealism becoming gangrened in later years and ultimately degenerating into a harsh contempt for

139

the general run of humanity. But to say that he was capable of deliberate "betrayal" is just so much my eye.

When three Labour leaders of such widely divergent temperaments as MacDonald, Snowden and Thomas decide to abandon the party they have belonged to all their lives, serious Socialists are bound to ask not what was wrong with their morals but what was wrong with their political philosophy.

All three men belonged to the "Socialism by Consent" school of socialists. That is, they accepted most of the assumptions of nineteenth-century liberalism. Every day, in every way, the world was to become better and better. There was to be no sharp, distressful struggle to decide whether economic power should remain a monopoly of a small group of overlords, or pass to the representatives of the people. Nothing like that. Simply a world more and more able to raise standards of living and bit by bit won over to the acceptance of each item in Labour's programme of social reforms. Can the Labour Movement assume that a Labour Government will ever be allowed to function in an atmosphere of trade prosperity and "confidence"? That 1929–31 was an entirely exceptional experience of a kind that will never again have to be faced? I don't think it can assume any such thing. But it does. And therein lies the tragedy of the present times. Labour has a policy for calm weather; no policy for crisis, in a world that is now in a permanent state of crisis.

I am writing in 1939, eight years after the downfall
of the Labour Government; eight years in which
fascism has come to power in Germany, Austria,
Czechoslovakia, Spain; but the British Labour Party
sleeps on. It still looks at the world obliquely through a
nineteenth-century mirror. It has not awakened to the
dangerous challenge of contemporary things. Perhaps
it is afraid to awake. Perhaps consciously or uncons-
ciously it knows that once it wakes a lovely dream will
be shattered for ever. The dream embodied in Mac-
Donald's early socialist writings. The dream that official
Labour still lives by. Belief in the possibility of Labour
Governments being allowed to carry through one piece
of social reform after another and so, gradually, step
by step, forward to socialism. The belief that the ruling
class of England will allow itself to be legislated out of
existence. It sounds incredible after its 1931 experiences and all that has happened in Europe since that
any vestige of that early faith should still remain.
But it does. And so far as it has died only fear seems
to have taken its place, fear expressing itself in bitter
hostility towards any socialist or group of socialists
who attempt to present a revised version of socialist
philosophy, strategy and economics more in keeping
with contemporary realities.

After the collapse of the Labour Government I wrote
to Sir Charles Trevelyan asking him about MacDonald
in Parliament during the war years. His reply confirmed what the best of our local socialists had always
maintained.

"As to J.R.M. I can't altogether disentangle my early and later feelings about him. I began very uncritical. I could not regard him as other than courageous. But I always found him avoiding straight issues. I was concerned with the U.D.C. He, Morel, Angel and I founded it. Certainly Morel and I did the chief of the work. Ramsay didn't hinder but didn't inspire. In the early part of the war he mostly lay low. In the House of Commons he took no part. During 1915 first Ponsonby, then I, then Snowden spoke. It required courage. I remember John Burns, a gallant, vain man, coming in and cheering me as if I were a popular leader, in a frigid house. It was a manly, human thing to do. And Asquith (quite justifiably) referred to the twittering of a sparrow in a hurricane.

"Such experience did not feed vanity in any way. Not till some time after did Ramsay speak. He thought he would be howled down. In that sense he was afraid. But I doubt if he was physically a coward. There were a few nasty meetings, and he at least went through with them. But he certainly hadn't the contemptuous indifference of Snowden, or Morel's challenging readiness to face contempt or death.

"Of course, his dominating anxiety was always not to make a decision. Every time our little band wanted to move and speak in the House of Commons he was against it. But Ponsonby, Snowden and I knew our minds and always got our way, and when the debates came he always spoke quite loyally and well. But we made the policy of peace by negotiation; he would

142

never have ventured it. I think during the war he had a certain courage. But I always have had a feeling that he was caught and felt it. He had expected to lead a big flock of Labour, perhaps international Labour, and there he was with a miserable remnant of stern pacifists. He wouldn't perhaps have done it if it had been to do again. That is what I feel about him.

"The vanity, which has now eaten away his soul, was in the first beginnings protective. He clung to what worship of him there was in those dark, cold days and got his solace there, where stronger men got it in the sense they were doing a damnably unpleasant job but less unpleasant than that of the poor devils in the trenches they were trying to save.

"If *his* speech at Glasgow was an oratorical success he glowed. If *mine* was a success, I could say 'thank God there are some of the people yet who are worth bearing the grim, political solitude for. Thank their good hearts and sane heads.'

"When fortune began to come his way, he knew himself for a really great man, which was his undoing. I am sure he deteriorated. For I cannot pretend to have had deeper doubts of him till I began to see him at work in the Cabinet, and clashed with him over the Zinoviev letter, and gasped at 'easy, oozy fools'."

MacDonald's desertion was spiritual death to thousands of Labour people who had worshipped him. That he should have left them was beyond comprehension.

I was not affected that way for I had grown up in

an environment intensely critical of MacDonald. Even his war record was regarded sceptically by many Fifeshire colliers. They declared that during the war Morel, Snowden, Trevelyan and others could be got to take any risk, speak anywhere, but MacDonald preferred to keep out of difficult areas until others had plunged in before him and tested the temperature.

The general body of Labour voters cannot be blamed for having trusted and adored the man. They saw only the fine actor declaiming his eloquent pieces. But those close to him and working within the party machine knew a very different MacDonald. In the end he was able to lead his party to disaster. For that the Parliamentary Labour Party of 1929–31 must carry a very heavy burden of responsibility.

Throughout the whole period of the Labour Government, a handful of us tried in vain to rouse our socialist colleagues to some sense of their individual responsibility.

In the Parliamentary Labour Party it was not the shepherds who frightened me. Nor yet the plain, ordinary party hacks. Every political party has a percentage of ambitious people ready to do anything that carries the hope of promotion. You are a fool if you don't expect to find that sort of thing and to have to reckon with it. I was prepared for that. But what I was totally unprepared for was the behaviour of the solid rows of decent, well-intentioned, unpretentious Labour back-benchers. In the long run it was they who did the most deadly damage. Again and again an effort was made to rouse them from their inertia. On every occasion they reacted like a load of damp cement. They would see nothing, do nothing, listen to nothing that had not first been given the seal of MacDonald's approval.

The I.L.P. group to which I belonged was bitterly attacked by the rest of the Labour Party for opposing the Government on the floor of the House. We were told that if we had any criticism to make, the place to raise our objections was in the private meetings of the Parliamentary Labour Party.

These meetings were the crowning ignominy of that unhappy time. Day after day MacDonald and Snowden were dragging us nearer disaster. The I.L.P. group protested. Sir Charles Trevelyan resigned from the Cabinet and in his speech of resignation baldly, without trimmings of any kind, informed his Parliamentary colleagues that they would do no good until they got rid of MacDonald. Sir Oswald Mosley and a few bright young men he had gathered around him carried on a separate guerrilla warfare on their own. But none of the dissenters had the least success. Baffled and furious more than once in those private meetings of the Party I found myself muttering Joe Corrie's "A' to Keep in Wi' the Gaffir".[1] That was probably very wicked of me. The majority of my colleagues may have genuinely agreed with the policy of MacDonald and Snowden. But if they did, just so

[1] A satirical poem after the style of the "Vicar of Bray." Written in collier dialect.

much more pitiful become their later denunciations of their leaders.

When the final collapse came the majority of Labour's supporters throughout the country did not see things my way. They refused to admit that MacDonald's crossing to the Tory benches was the end of a process. They preferred to regard it as an isolated and infamous act. In a howl of bitter execration, they called for MacDonald's blood. MacDonald's old henchmen obligingly stepped forward and led them in the burning of his effigy. That was the cheapest and safest thing for them to do. Much easier than facing up to a serious analysis of what had gone wrong, to a recognition that MacDonald's defection was merely a superficial by-product; that the causes of Labour's failure went much deeper than that. The first time I voted against the Labour Government I did so with the greatest reluctance. The I.L.P. group magnificently led by John Wheatley (whose death was a major political tragedy for the whole socialist movement, not just for the small group of us who were most closely associated with him) set itself up as a kind of unofficial opposition to MacDonald. It did so from the very first days of the Labour Government. I thought that unfair. "Give them time," I urged. "Give them a chance. The Government is dependent on liberal votes before it can pass a single piece of legislation. Its hands are tied. It is unreasonable to expect too much. Perhaps the Cabinet has some sort of plan and is manœuvring for the right moment to bring it forward."

But the summer months dragged on, winter came, the unemployed were as badly off as ever, no serious work schemes were attempted and we were all supposed to pin our faith to the increasingly tenuous utterances of Mr. Ramsay MacDonald.

At first I had voted against the Government rather gingerly and with considerable doubts as to whether or not that was the right thing to do. But I became increasingly convinced that there was no effective answer to those who claimed that what such a Government did not attempt in its first months of office, it would not do at all. I knew all the careful arguments that the party managers could muster for avoiding at all costs the defeat of the Government until it had had a run for several years. A second general election within a year or eighteen months of the last meant a terrific strain on the Party's finances. That was serious. But there were worse calamities. I believe in teaching by doing. The great mass of people are not politically minded. I wanted to see the Labour Party attempt something concrete and understandable. I did not mind which of a number of things it was—nationalization of mines, fulfilment of election pledges to the unemployed, or say, to old-age pensioners. The onus would then lie with the Liberal Party either to give the Government the necessary majority or explain to the country why it had refused to do so. I did not even feel certain that a quick, firm stand of that kind would have brought in profitable party dividends, measured in terms of votes, at the election that might have been

147

precipitated. But again, it did not seem to me the job of a Socialist Party always to trim its sails so that it might in all circumstances win the maximum number of votes. People have to learn by experience. If another Tory Government got itself elected in the midst of the world-wide economic depression of 1930–31, I did not see that that need have been the end of the world or even of the Labour Party. The country would have been left with the memory of a straightforward, honourable effort on the part of Labour to fulfil its election promises. That memory would have stood Labour in good stead when people were once again in the mood to turn our way. There is no shame in fighting and being overcome by superior numbers. Shame comes when a party refuses to fight, however elaborate the reasons it may produce for running away.

If MacDonald had had a sense of humour, you might have thought it was some puckish whim on his part that made him appoint Mr. J. H. Thomas as a kind of emergency Minister of Action to deal with unemployment, giving him Sir Oswald Mosley and George Lansbury as his assistants. That was one of the Prime Minister's many stalling devices. Nothing got done, but the new appointment sounded fine, made a useful talking point for a month or two and kept the wolves of reality from the door. If J. H. Thomas had not been an important and influential Labour leader I would have found him good fun. He was a merry scamp. When I met him in the evenings bulging out of his dress shirt I could never help grinning. He looked so exactly like the caricatures of himself that you had to prod him to see if he were real. It would have been all very funny if there had not been millions of destitute people desperate for work and looking to him to make some serious effort to meet their needs. But that was something that neither he nor his Cabinet colleagues seemed able or willing to do. I watched Sir Oswald Mosley ably assisted by John Strachey try again and again to break through the Government's inertia. Failing to make any headway, Mosley next tried campaigning among private members of the Parliamentary party. He had not the least success. What MacDonald did not initiate or at least sanction, the Faithful would not even consider. Very likely Mosley's insane vanity would have attracted him towards the role of fascist *Führer* even without his experiences within the Labour Party. But I wish that the blistering contempt that he developed around 1930 for the "yes" men with whom MacDonald surrounded himself, had had less to justify it. Mosley's wealth and arrogance fenced him off from the ordinary worthwhile dependable rank and file of the Labour Movement. He knew next to nothing of this, the Party's greatest asset. He knew everything there was to know about its liabilities, about the tired, cynical, profoundly reactionary elements that occupy an alarmingly high percentage of official posts. Mosley had no roots in the working-class movement. It was emotionally as easy for him to leave it as it had been for him to join it. There was nothing in his memories, values, traditional loyalties to prevent him buying himself a black shirt, a bodyguard and setting out to indulge his spleen against the whole socialist movement, and everyone and everything associated with it, to the last bitter dregs.

The small I.L.P. group with which I worked during the period of the Labour Government, had as little to do with Mosley as with MacDonald. We shied suspiciously at the approach of both. But we were keenly concerned to see the Labour Government make some attempt to keep its work or maintenance pledge to the unemployed. Private Members of Parliament and groups of Members deluged Mr. J. H. Thomas's department with suggestions for work schemes. Many of these proposals may have been impracticable. Mr. J. H. Thomas assured us all of them were. He negatived almost every suggestion. And put very little in their place.

It was this negativing propensity of the Labour Government that tried everyone inside the Parliamentary Labour Party who was energetic and concerned more sorely than anything else. It drove everyone under forty to the verge of madness. We all went off at a tangent. Mosley, Dr. Forgan, John Beckett to fascism. John Strachey to communism, Oliver Baldwin and W. J. Brown to positions as independents, myself to a disaffiliated I.L.P.

Aneurin Bevan was about the only one of the younger Members with a sound anti-inertia record who remained within the official machine. He argued day and night with John Strachey and myself in an effort to make us do likewise. At that time Strachey had committed himself to co-operating with Mosley in forming the New Party. Bevan argued vociferously against this course. "Where is the money coming from?" he demanded. "Who is going to pay? Who is going to call the tune? I tell you now where you will end up. You will end up as a fascist party. I tell you——"

Then turning to me—I was bent on what I called "keeping faith" with the best of our Scottish I.L.P. even to the point of remaining with them if they should decide to leave the Labour Party—"And as for you, I tell you what the epitaph of you Scottish dissenters is going to be—pure, but impotent. Yes, you will be pure all right. But remember, at the price of impotency. You will not influence the course of British politics by as much as a hair's-breadth. Why don't you get into a nunnery and be done with it? Lock yourself up in a separate cell away from the world and its wickedness. My Salvation Army lassie. Poor little Casabianca. That was a hell of an intelligent performance now, wasn't it? I tell you, it is the Labour Party or nothing. I know all its faults, all its dangers. But it is the party that we have taught millions of working people to look to and regard as their own. We can't undo what we have done. And I am by no means convinced that something cannot yet be made of it." I had many other friends inside the Labour Party who made the same sort of appeal to me. I tried

151

hard to school myself to respond. But a sick feeling in the pit of my stomach held me back.

It was true that some of those with whom I was asked to associate in rebuilding the public's faith in our *bona-fides* were fine, honourable men and women with a self-forgetful devotion to the cause of socialism. But an uncomfortable number of the others seemed to me quite empty inside. They dared not disbelieve in public for believing was their trade. But in private their cynicism chilled everything they touched with the stale atmosphere of decay.

CHAPTER IX

IN the November 1931 election when the Mac-
Donald-Baldwin "National Government" was returned, I, in common with so many other socialist
candidates, was defeated at the polls. I had to make up
my mind what I intended to do next. There was
nothing I wanted to do. Nothing, that is, except read,
take time for reflection, renew contacts with the
rank-and-file of the Scottish movement, find out how
much human material was available for starting all
over again. I still believed that we could build a
socialist movement that not only talked about winning
power, but really wanted power and would know what
to do with it once it had it. This "nothing", therefore,
was a full time, exhausting occupation.

But it did not provide any salary. It required me to
find money elsewhere to pay for food and lodgings. I
had to unearth, therefore, some kind of side-line so
that my stomach might sustain me while my convictions were trying to sustain the tattered remnants of
our I.L.P.

It was under these compulsions that I first approached America. Long before my time Labour
notables, large and small, had established a regular

trade route between Great Britain and the States. Old hands put me "wise" to the ropes. First, you find an agent who will advertise your wares. It is the agent's job to approach the infinite number of colleges, town forums, foreign policy associations, women's clubs, men's clubs, peace groups and the rest in which America abounds, inquiring who wants to have you come to lecture to them and how much are they prepared to pay. The agent deducts his commission, and you pay all your travelling expenses and, if you are lucky—if—you return home with the trade balance in your favour.

The fortunes of the American lecture world are, to say the least, varied. Socialists, anarchists, communists, liberals, fascists, conservatives and republicans from every corner of the globe jostle one another for the ear of the American public.

An agent's job is a highly-skilled affair. He knows how to build up the right kind of "story" about each new prodigy in turn. Americans like piquancy and, if you go there to lecture, you are going to be made piquant whether you like it or not. I found, to my infinite embarrassment, that wherever I went I was resplendently introduced in terms that almost knocked me unconscious.

I had been speaking from coal carts at an age when other children are still in their cradles. I was Hypatia, Portia and Jenny Geddes all in one. I was the youngest woman ever to have been elected to the British House of Commons.

If I had been the fattest woman who had ever swum the Atlantic, or the saltiest sailor who had ever climbed to the top of the North Pole, I could not have been more highly acclaimed.

This phase did not last long. I rapidly deteriorated in market value and on the last occasion I visited America, was thrown around the country at cut-rate bargain prices.

No ordinary commercial agent could be expected to put up with me. I was constantly falling through the hoop and landing on my behind beside a group of striking miners, or in Uncle Tom's Cabin where he and I and all his coloured family had a grand old time together. But there was no money in it!

I loved the south. When you arrive in Memphis, the soft husky voices ask if you are going to the "deep" south. The "deep" south! I liked the sweet tang of that. It means down to New Orleans. And so I was. I was prepared to go down just as deep as they could make it.

Cortes, "silent upon a peak in Darien," was not more pleased with himself than I was first time I pene- trated as far south as the Gulf of Mexico. It was February and, by all my northern standards, it ought to have been cold and disagreeable. Instead, the world was a festival of sunshine and flowers, scarlet and purple and gold, flaunting ones, gentle ones. I know very few flowers by name. But I know lots of them by their character. My idea of wealth is to have masses of flowers.

In the Gulf of Mexico in February, I felt like an illegitimate millionaire. I was rolling in wealth and all at the wrong time of the year too!

But I doubt if I should have loved the south so much if I had just regarded it as a spectacle. It was its people that held me most. It was the coloured people and their unaffected ways and their quick laughter and their brown skins and their plentiful piccaninnies and their voices and their songs. And, tying us in close fraternity, the pathos of their tentative first efforts to organize industrial unions.

At Mark Tree, about two hours' car ride from Memphis, I had my sharpest taste of the bitter behind the sweet of this deluding south.

In the early months of the year the cotton plantations are brown and bare. The only things that catch the eye are the tumble-down wooden shacks dotted about the fields, some of them hanging at such an angle that you hold your breath, waiting for them to fall over.

White families live in some. Coloured folks in others. They are all share-croppers and all nakedly poor. We had come out to form a union and to invite black workers and white workers and workers of all the shades in between, to join together in the one organization. But the Sheriff and his thugs decided no meeting should be permitted. At the edge of the town we were met and warned off.

The group of poor, white share-croppers who were waiting for us, were downcast at the news. We looked at one another, I trying to sense what to say. I was keen to go on with the meeting, but conscious of my safe British passport tucked inside my dispatch-case. I was just a passer-by. It was the local people who would have to suffer any consequences.

When labour trouble breaks out in the south, you can get shot and you can get beaten up. A young union organizer was killed in this area a short time after this. But those seemed remote possibilities. More likely I might, at worst, be gaoled for a night—that is nothing in America. It happens more often and means less than it would in this country.—But if gaoled or deported the story would be "news". It would be featured in the press. It would bring down on my head profitable invitations from well-to-do lecture organizations to come and tell them all about it. I could not quite put my finger on it, but there seemed to me to be something wrong in that sort of alignment. But America is like that. One-half is always anxious to pay you for lecturing to it about things that the other half wants to gaol or deport you for.

When I explained my scruples to the local committee, they were jubilant. They had been hesitating only on my account. If I was game to speak then, somehow, they would fix up a meeting.

The compromise they made, in face of the Sheriff and his gunmen, was to drive a lorry into the fields just outside the boundaries of the town, then the word was sent round that it was there we were going to meet.

I stood by the side of the lorry watching the crowd assemble. From all points of the compass, the outcasts of the south came slowly towards us. At first in twos and threes. Then in larger numbers. Some were white. Most were coloured. Around the lorry they were jumbled up all together. It was time now for the meeting to begin. Presiding over our meeting, to my infinite delight, we had old Uncle Tom himself. He had on his frayed, black frock-coat and his benevolent air just as I had pictured him in my childhood's story-book.

He opened the meeting with prayer. He blessed the meeting and blessed the union and blessed the town and blessed the president. I think even God was given his blessing. He was followed by the Union organizer, who briefly explained the purpose for which we had met.

Another stranger, who had blown in from some-where, was Naomi Mitchison. Naomi, rather breath-less, fervent and kind, as always, was asked to speak for five minutes.

I don't think those simple children of the south under-stood much of what she said, but they felt that she was all right and counted her in.

It was now my turn. What an audience! I had met nothing like it. We could easily have worked upon one another's feelings until we became a kind of political holy rollers. I held myself in check as well as I could. When I concluded, the audience, which had been standing all the time, seemed to rise. Raising its arms heavenwards, it chanted in unison a hymn of union solidarity:

> *We will not be moved,*
> *We will not be moved,*
> *Like a tree, planted by the river,*
> *We—will not—be moved.*

That was the general refrain, repeated with infinite variations and going all the way up and down the keyboard. It was their own language. It was a negro-spiritual. It was their own inimitable way of saying that they would stand by one another and not allow themselves to be intimidated. And it was sung as only angels and negro plantation workers know how.

After that, the whole demonstration walking two by two, the platform party leading, moved slowly towards the town. We walked warily, singing the union hymn and watching for the Sheriff and his men.

That day they did not interfere. They let us pass. So I had to wait until I was among white workers, entirely and exclusively white, before I saw America's rawest side.

I had heard of Harlem County, the coalfield where no union was tolerated, where the coal companies openly employed armed thugs and where any man or woman who dared challenge their authority was shot or gaoled or beaten up and run out over the county line.

All that is an old story to Americans, and I hear that John L. Lewis, backed by President Roosevelt, has come to the aid of miners who, in such areas, attempt to organize in defiance of company batons and company guns.

But in 1932 President Roosevelt was not yet on the map. The class war was being waged in the Kentucky mining-camps without even a loin-cloth around its middle.

Quite alone, a mere observer, I arrived in Harlem. Within an hour, two ruffians broke into my hotel bedroom. I was talking with the wife of one of the local miners' leaders. It was the miner himself I had expected to meet, but he had been beaten up and thrown over the county line shortly before I arrived.

One of the two invaders lurched forward, attempted to grip my wrist and snarled, "I guess we'll keep you." They were disgusting-looking toughs, and it was all so like a badly-acted improbable Hollywood production that my fury was tempered with disbelief. No, this was not real. This was a caricature of reality.

The voice of the outraged Britisher—it has its uses if you don't happen to be up against your own authorities—held them back. I ordered them to give me an account of who they were and what they thought they were doing.

One explained that he was the mayor of the town. The other that he was the chief of the police. Both chorussed that they had been told I was another goddam reporter from New York and that they had had enough of other people nosing into their affairs. They were sorry, lady, but they had to keep the town in order. There were a lot of tough characters around.

Afterwards, with these two guardians of law and order at my heels, I went on a sightseeing expedition. At the local gaol I was able to get into communication with some of our organizers, a young Y.W.C.A. secretary and a reporter or two, who, sure enough, were all tidily locked up inside.

Next day I contrived to get off on my own to the mining settlements a few miles outside the town. There I found families living in a pre-Truck Act age, with the company store flourishing and a starving and terrorized community answering violence with violence, for nothing else was allowed it.

Later, I met the miners of Gillespie, Illinois. Compared with Kentucky they seemed peaceful and prosperous. But, if you go among them, they too can tell you stories of the class war fought out fist for fist and gun for gun.

I had no thought of going to Gillespie until the miners themselves sent repeated messages insisting that I must. Then, at last, I went—laugh if you like—because I heard that one of the Gillespie miners had worked beside my father in Lochgelly and others had emigrated from our part of Fife. We had a boisterous time together. A packed public meeting, a feast in the village hall, a presentation from the children, another from the grown-ups and, later in the evening, when we gathered in one of the miner's houses—there was no fireside to sit around, but everything else was home-like—what tales! what tales! Lochgelly battles, Gillespie battles, all fought over again, with the children listening-in as I in my own home so often had listened, to this, their own, superb and little recorded history.

There is a great deal more on the other side of the Atlantic besides mining-camps and cotton-plantations. Even I could not help but notice that. The eager, restless mood of great masses of Americans is for ever sweeping them off in half a dozen contradictory directions at once. But, at least, they sweep. They don't stagnate. I could never quite make up my mind whether this was the finest or the damnedst country in the world. It has wide islands of civilized living, then plomp, down you plunge into raging currents of savagery.

There are flags of freedom flying higher and wider in America than anywhere else in the world. A glorious breeze blows through corners of the press. I saw God and the Statue of Liberty impersonated on the New York stage. After New York, London theatres are intolerably dull. Nothing is allowed. The censor does his best to reduce every performance to the stale uniformity of the Berlin theatres. If you want to see anything that is even worth comparing with "Green Pastures" or "Of Thee I Sing", you have to go to small private theatres.

I totally failed to form any coherent picture of America. I don't think it can be done. And the more Americans explained America to me, the more blurred the pattern became.

On the evening I arrived in New York, Maurice Hindus took me to a party. Everybody who writes books in the whole of America seemed to be there. It was probably all very pleasant but so hot and crammed and noisy that I wanted to go home. Maurice was enjoying himself among friends. He had no intention of taking me home. Instead he piloted me from one group of fierce conversationalists to another, ending up in the corner of the room where Sinclair Lewis had betaken himself. I was nicely introduced and for at least the tenth time that evening had America explained to me. But this time I got something to hold on to. I was interested and entertained, for Sinclair Lewis talked about his country in the way that a younger and more aggressive David Kirkwood used to talk about Scotland: a kick and a caress comically mixed up together in every sentence.

At lunch the following day Walter Lippman gave me a much more formal school text-book sketch of the U.S.A. I had to remember that each State was a law unto itself, that the federal principle meant a total lack of uniformity, that I could go out and find whatever I set out to find, beauty, terror, fine living, unbeatable squalor. And, above all, I had to remember that America had drawn its population from every part of the world. That, in itself, presented terrific educational and economic problems.

And so ding-dong, one after the other, all crammed into my first week on the other side of the Atlantic, I listened to representative Americans describing their country.

It is, maybe, just perversity on my part, but it was

those of them who made no attempt at all at official flag-waving who left me with the best feeling towards America. I am thinking of men like Norman Thomas, Scott Nearing, Roger Baldwin, Professor John Dewey, Garfield Hays, John Dos Passos. I listened to their criticisms of the society they lived in but also took note that they too were part of that society. That evened things up quite a bit.

When I was ready to return to England a telegram arrived for me from the idealistic young man, who, at that time, was secretary of the National Canadian Clubs. It was an invitation to spend a month in Canada as the guest-speaker of the clubs. I had plenty of free time just then so I wired back saying I was on my way.

Once in Ottawa I found it difficult to know whether I was standing on my head or my heels; whether to treat the whole affair seriously or as a huge joke. For there I was, dumped solemnly in the centre of an enormous stuffed-shirt type of luncheon party with the then Prime Minister, Mr. W. B. Bennett, on my right hand, and Mr. Mackenzie King on my left. Someone, just before we took our seats, whispered to me that the two men had no affection for one another. It was to be up to me to keep everything going nicely.

When everyone had reached the coffee and cigarettes stage the president announced that I would now give a lecture on "The Younger Generation in Soviet Russia". And so I did. Very willingly. It was evident that Russia had few friends in that very official assembly. Because of that I praised it all the more ardently. If the U.S.S.R. lives up to just one-tenth of what I promised in its name, it will be doing very well indeed.

A bit alarmed by the luncheon I decided I had better find out what sort of jamboree this was that I had let myself in for. What was it all about? Why had I been asked?

I got hold of the idealistic young secretary. Looking a bit reckless, worried and rather pleased all in one, he explained. The club was a non-party association. Its guest-speakers from England were usually high Tories or Liberals. He had got the idea that having heard Tory and Liberal versions of European affairs over and over again, it was only fair that club members should now hear what a British socialist had to say. So here I was.

That seemed to me reasonable enough. So I set off across Canada. And even within the carefully cotton-woolled atmosphere of the clubs I met many fine people who helped me to see a good deal of the real working life of their country.

I don't keep a diary and have forgotten the name of the small agricultural centre somewhere to the west of Lake Winnipeg, where I spent my pleasantest evening under club auspices. But I don't forget the gathering of working farmers and their wives and families who were my hosts that evening. I had wandered a long way from the formal atmosphere of Ottawa.

That was in the winter of 1932. Canada, like the rest of the world, was in the doldrums. Its poorer farmers were going through hell. But that particular evening they were bent on forgetting their cares, and one after another drove up in their antiquated Fords and still more antiquated buggies to a barn-like building that had been made into a banquet hall for the occasion. It was to be a supper-party, a dance, a sing-song and a meeting all in one. Someone had put a small piece of heather on my plate. I was the guest of honour. They intended to do me proud.

I heard good radical talk that evening. But what I remember best is the way we all stood up around the great supper-table and how much I enjoyed myself when instead of the usual pious national anthem there came thundering about my ears a chorus that went something like this: "Hor-sie, keep your tail up, keep your tail up, keep your tail up,—Horsie, keep your tail up,—When the spring comes you'll get corn."

You need the noise and the tune and the atmosphere before you can catch on to what it was all about. The song and the singing were just a bit of fun. Part of the jollifications. No one tried to draw tiresome morals. But I am certain the reason why I remember them so especially was that both at the time and in looking back they seemed to me a pretty good summary of the lives of the people I had wandered in among.

But it was the wild geese who came flocking to meet me wherever I went who taught me most about Canada. People from the derelict parts of Scotland,

166

people without money, without influence, uprooted from their former homes because there was no work for them there and now finding Canada's welcome colder than its coldest winter day.

One of the sights to be seen in most Canadian cities that winter were the queues where unemployed men lined up for food rations. I was taken along to have a look at them. I am not good at that kind of sight-seeing; stepping forward squired by the official in charge; invited to taste the soup to see for yourself that it is not at all bad. You need a tough skin to do that kind of thing well. I found myself averting my eyes from the long line of shabby men standing quietly and patiently waiting for food. Why should I invade their privacy? Stare at them as if they were so many animals on parade?

How would I like to be stared at if I were standing in such a queue? But it was a different matter when two of the unemployed men started signalling to me and I turned and saw who they were. They were old friends. They had worked with me in the North Lanark by-election. So we got together and first they insisted on hearing all my news, then they started telling me about themselves. They were willing enough to talk— but on terms. I had to promise that when I went back to Scotland if I met any of their relations I would not "let on" how and where I had met them. They were down on their luck, but they would get over it "and there is no sense, see Jennie, in worrying ma mither!"

It was the same old story, wild geese on the wing and wanted nowhere. In Canada families that had been ratepayers in a fixed place for a certain number of years then found themselves out of work, had a chance of being provided for in a bald kind of way. But no place would accept responsibility for newcomers. Recent immigrants had the worst time of all. If they arrived in a town in search of employment they might be permitted to sleep there overnight (as likely as not housed in the local gaol) but in the morning they had to move on. If they looked like giving "trouble" a police-escort accompanied them to the city boundaries.

It is a crazy world. At that time we were all already being deafened by the German and Japanese clamour for more territory. Poor little Japan (so it said) could not feed its teeming millions through lack of land. (But it could afford to maintain a most expensive military caste and a fantastically costly arms equipment!) Germany the same. Both governments howled, give us more space and we will make our people happy and prosperous.

Well, here was Canada, 3,694,843 square miles, a population of under twelve millions, short of colonizing the moon no state could hope to have more territory at its disposal, yet wherever I went I was finding poverty and unemployment.

Canada must always remain for me an unsatisfactory jumble of irreconcilable elements. It treated me as a privileged guest. Club officials, labour members of Parliament, even its very conservative Prime Minister,

seemed to take a paternal interest in seeing that I
missed nothing they considered worth seeing. I don't
forget and I am not ungrateful. If a little flattery and a
lot of spoiling could blind the eyes and still the tongue,
all I need do is curtsey nicely and say thank you very
much, I enjoyed the party. But the wild geese who
gave me their unofficial welcome wherever I went
meant more to me than all the rest. I had known some
of them in Scotland. Others who came to my meetings
or found other ways of getting in touch with me had
never met me before but perhaps knew the district I came
from, or perhaps just wanted to hear a Scotch voice or
to ask about places and people that had once been their
whole life. Sometimes just to shake hands and hurry
away blinded by tears.

I hate the foul business of a nation pretending to be
just one nice big family when it is no such thing. No
class society can be a reputable "family". All that
happens is that well-to-do patriots sing their own
praises so loudly that they cannot even hear the cry of
those they are trampling underfoot. And if at any
moment the cries of the poor threaten to drown the
Hallelujah chorus of the prosperous, then legislation is
rushed through Parliament (if it is not already on the
statute book), the soldiers and the police are brought
out, a "state of emergency" is declared, and at the
wrong end of a machine-gun if need be, the poor are
taught that it is dangerous even to complain.

I did not, of course, need to cross the Atlantic to
learn anything so elementary. But a new setting, new

situations, underlined the old problems that I had lived with all my life. I was eager to be home again. I have a lot of restlessness in me. I like travelling, new places, new people, new experiences. But, best of all, I like the return journey, the coming back to where you have roots that go very deep down into the earth, the coming back to familiar places and people. I have heard it said that that is a collier trait; that we have this homing instinct more strongly than most. I don't believe it. I think most people have the same need. I think one of the most ghastly sorrows in the world to-day is the tragedy of the millions of people who, because they are poor or because they are Jews or because of their politics or religion can find harbourage nowhere. Uprooted, unwanted, wild geese flapping their pitiful wings from country to country.

I am totally incapable of parcelling out these unfortunates into separate groups. They are all part of a common indictment against the economic and cultural values of capitalist society.

Nowadays I don't use abstract words such as capitalist, socialist, fascist, democratic any oftener than I can help. I am profoundly distrustful of them. For each of us, according to our social background and political leanings, means something different when we use such terms. I wish politicians would stop using them altogether. That would not of itself solve any of our problems. But if, instead, they would use concrete and particular language, we might at least begin to understand what our problems are. You can quarrel for ever over an abstract phrase and not even come to any common agreement as to what it is that you are quarrelling about.

The later chapters of this book would be easier for me to write if I had not such a hearty dislike of abstract generalizations that can mean anything or nothing. And that covers a great deal of current political jargon. Take the word "socialism", for instance. At one time I was for ever using it. In my own mind I gave it exact and satisfactory content. I thought it quite all right to use it as a kind of shorthand to indicate the economic and cultural values I would like to see governing the world. But it has since been dirtied by every kind of contemptible and equivocal usage.

Hitler borrowed it for the name of his party. MacDonald clung to it to the end of his life. The Labour Party swears by it and, at the same time, by the King and the Royal Family and knighthoods for Labour leaders and full compensation even for millionaires with shares in any industry a future Labour Government might venture to nationalize.

Hitler, MacDonald, the official manifestoes of the British Labour Party, may interpret the word correctly. But if they do I have been using it falsely all my life and just haven't the faintest notion as to what it actually means.

I think, therefore, I had better continue to tell a rather personal story, hoping that in the telling, by the time I catch up with the present, it may all sum up to give at least some general notion of the compulsions that have driven me to write at all. But I cannot be sure of that. I must take the risk. And anyhow, for a bit yet, it is not so difficult for me to write on. For I am looking back seven years, which is almost the same as saying, looking back to life on another planet.

CHAPTER X

IN 1932 most of us still felt we could plan for the future, be leisurely and casual, wilful and unconcerned. There was not the present grim tension in the air. But even then the atmosphere was quite tense enough for those of us who by temperament and circumstance were keenly involved in political happenings. Politics, for me, means the fight against poverty. That is what it meant to working people in the days of the Chartist agitations. That is what it has always meant and always will mean. Well-to-do liberals find it very hard to understand that. Sometimes they totally fail to do so and when and where that happens, poor people betray them to fascism. For libertarian principles, "democracy", "civil liberties", lose all vitality whenever an attempt is made to call a truce in the fight against poverty. Poor people look on political liberties primarily as instruments to be used in fighting their economic battles. Democratic institutions used aggressively on their behalf can count on their allegiance. But they are just not interested in a passive kind of democracy that expects them to put up quietly with a ten-shilling old-age pension, means tests, and slums.

The main source of my disillusionment with the

Labour Government of 1929–31 was that it was far too half-hearted and apologetic in fighting the battles of the poor.

I expected nothing from Tory governments so they had no power to wound me. But for me a Labour Government was a very different matter.

When I got back from America in the spring of 1932 I was still in a mood of violent revulsion at the memory of how shabbily poor people had been treated by the Government they had worked so hard to create. I knew all the official excuses: none of them satisfied me.

All the same, when the Independent Labour Party at its annual conference that same year decided to break off all organizational contact with the Labour Party, I had considerable misgivings as to whether or not that was a wise thing to do.

I envied some of my I.L.P. friends who were able to see the whole situation in terms of biblical simplicity. For them it was as uncomplicated as a Passion Play. It was a struggle between Right and Wrong, Good and Evil. The Labour Party had become in their eyes a kind of political anti-Christ. It besmirched, it betrayed, the True Faith.

I was intellectually impatient of that kind of mumbo-jumbo, but emotionally a good deal under its influence. I did not want to leave the Labour Party. But I did not see how I could do otherwise. I did not see how I could go on making socialist speeches for a party some of whose leaders I was as much out at elbows with as I had been with MacDonald, whose programme I could accept only with considerable reservations and whose structure was such that it was arithmetically impossible to amend either its leadership or its policy however hard one might campaign inside the local Labour Parties.

It was that last point I stuck on more than any other. It is so important and explains so much that may seem mysterious to the outsider trying to understand how to account for the behaviour of the British working-class movement that I want to return to it later in greater detail. I did not want to leave the Labour Party. I dreaded the kind of dog fight that was bound to develop in North Lanark once rival I.L.P. and Labour Party candidates took the field. I longed for a nice, easy, straightforward political situation in which there would be two great parties in the State and only two. The workers *versus* the rest. I had taken it for granted in all my growing years that my special job in life was to fight coalowners and all they stand for. I loved that particular fight. It raised no divisions inside myself. It was unanswerably, triumphantly worthwhile. It was a fight for bread. It was more than that. It was a fight for status too. My grandfather and my father were proud men. So were their workmates. The thought of them as under-dogs, mere work-beasts labouring for the greater glory and profit of a caste-ridden plutocracy was intolerable. And such a plutocracy! It gave us 1914–18. Families like mine tried to stop the butchering. It gave us the vindictive reparation clauses of the Versailles Treaty. Families like mine tried to curb their rulers' greed. About ten years too late Britain's most distinguished economists began to talk a language that Fife colliers had made me familiar with while the post-war world was still in the making; while Germany could still have been securely won as a friend, a good neighbour, an invaluable ally in lifting to unprecedented new levels the whole standard of European life. Our people were wiser than all the pretentious highly-placed "experts" who made such a parade of their learning. Their daily experiences made them so. They knew it was nonsense to talk of squeezing Germany until the pip squeaks. And they knew, too, humane considerations apart, that it was bad economics. Reparations paid in German coal might make the distribution of wealth between nations and within nations just a little more crazily lopsided than it already was. But what good would it do to the over-worked underpaid German collier? Or to the British collier idle and hungry because his former market was being glutted by supplies from the Ruhr?

I did not want to leave the Labour Party. I wanted to take part in a political contest where the alignments were as energizingly simple as the one penny fairy-tale and two comic-cuts that had delighted my childhood. I wanted to slay all the dragons and set poor people free. I wanted it to be All of Us *versus* The Others.

But in 1932 the British working-class movement was in no mood to accommodate me. It had split into warring factions. Tempers were brittle and hearts sore with the memory of how utterly, abysmally, Mac-Donald and his Cabinet had failed. I had to choose. It had to be either Labour Party or I.L.P. It could not be both.

One of the ironies of that 1932 situation was that those who had been closest to MacDonald and who, after he left the Labour Party stepped into leadership positions, immediately opened fire on those of us who had warned the movement where it was drifting, who had dared criticize the Labour Government, and who, again and again had even voted against it. I found myself presented with an ultimatum. I was ordered to put my signature to a document in which I had to promise that I would never again "misbehave" in the future as I had done in the past. The "misbehaviour" in question being that I had found out MacDonald before they did and had dared to oppose the policies that led us to disaster. North Lanark Divisional Labour Party wrote inviting me to continue as Parliamentary Candidate for the division. But the condition they laid down was—I had to sign on the dotted line. I tried hard to bring myself to the point of signing. But, ultimately, the reply I sent was as follows: (It was written at a time when I still assumed that the word "socialist" was self-explanatory.)

12 *Paul Street*,
Lochgelly,
Fife.
5*th August*, 1932.

Dear Mr. Lashley,

I have received a letter from the Secretary of Shotts Labour Party inviting me to accept nomination as prospective Labour Candidate for North Lanark, but regret it is not possible for me to do so.

In view of the three contests we have put through together and the devoted service that workers of every shade of Labour opinion have given in order to make the work of a Labour and Socialist Movement possible throughout the Division, I am anxious through you to make clear the reasons that force me to take this difficult and unpleasant stand. I have no personal grievances whatsoever against the Labour Party. It has showered kindnesses and opportunities of every kind upon me, and if at this moment I were consulting my own comfort and convenience, I should most certainly remain with the larger and more powerful organization.

But, as a socialist, it is quite impossible for me to give the written promises that are being demanded by the Labour Party as a condition of endorsement. I am more than willing to promise to support any future Labour Government so far as it is carrying out our socialist policy. But that promise will not be accepted by Party Headquarters. They are demanding that here and now I pledge myself to give unqualified support to any future Labour Cabinet irrespective of who may compose that Cabinet or what its policy may be. That I cannot do. It would be cowardly and hypocritical on my part to pretend that I can. So far as a Labour Cabinet is carrying out socialist policy the question of my loyalty does not arise. But if ever again a Labour Cabinet asked me to vote for Tory unemployment commissions and economy committees that I felt sure would produce reports to be used against the workers and unemployed, nothing would induce me to act otherwise than I did in the last Parliament. I stated my difficulty in this respect to high officials within the Labour Party and they replied that I had always the right to abstain from voting. That right is not enough. If a Labour Cabinet or any other Cabinet produces legislation that means reduced wages or worsened conditions for any section of workers, no socialist has the right to remain merely neutral. I must be free to support the socialist alternatives in keeping with pre-election promises and propaganda. That right I am definitely and categorically denied.

Hence I must carry on my socialist work outside the Labour Party. If I remained inside, I should feel every socialist speech I made a form of fraud. Any intelligent worker would be entitled to ask me if I could be trusted to act and vote as I spoke, and in reply to such a question I should be compelled to admit that I had already promised one hundred per cent obedience to any future Labour Government so that he could have no guarantee that I might not vote contrary to any-

179

thing I might say. I know no way of evading this point. If socialists are prepared to sign pledges that they do not really believe in, in order to save themselves from embarrassments and splits, then we cannot blame the ordinary worker if he becomes sceptical and distrusting of all of us, arguing that if we are willing to act so in such issues, he can have no certainty of our stability in other things.

I deeply regret that after the failure of the late Labour Government to stick to socialist policy the party machine is not directing its energies at present towards devising rules that would compel both Cabinet ministers and rank and file members in the future to stand by socialist policy and would deal promptly and effectively with any attempt to compromise the party by feeble or anti-socialist legislation. That I believe would have brought real unity to the movement and a sense that we really were preparing to make a serious socialist challenge to capitalism. The responsibility of the Labour Party in taking an exactly opposite course and forcing socialists to leave it at this moment rather than give up their right to vote and act as socialists as well as *talk* socialism, is a grave one. I can assure you that I hate and deplore the necessity of leaving the Labour Party, but hope that every socialist will do likewise rather than carry on a semblance of false unity when no real common purpose and intention remains.

May I express my gratitude and appreciation of the work that has been done by scores of good comrades in every part of the Division to make a Labour and socialist movement possible. I am fully conscious of the trust that North Lanark was prepared to put in me at an age that made the rest of the country gasp, and hope to go on attempting to justify that trust by doing what my socialist faith compels me to do.

I know that in 1926 when I helped to get Mac-Donald out of the I.L.P., many older people cried out treason and folly. I know that in the late Parliament the votes that I gave against wage-cuts and Tory economy committees were criticized and deplored at the time, although supported later. In the present issue I am convinced that time will once more be on my side.

A united working class is essential for the achievement of socialism but the preliminary to such real unity is that both high and low are pledged to carry out socialist policy. Such a pledge the Labour movement is not asking and will not accept. Instead it asks me to support future governments whether they act for or against socialist policy.

That I cannot do, so I must work elsewhere for the creation of a real socialist movement and hope in doing so to have the support of all workers who are more concerned about socialist action and principles than about an autocratic enforcement of rigid rules of discipline compelling acceptance of what might well prove as ineffective legislation as that of the last Parliament.

Yours sincerely,
JENNIE LEE.

Once my letter was in the post I felt very naked.
The door-bell rang. When I saw Aneurin Bevan outside I had half a mind to pretend that I was not at
home. But I had better get it over. I knew what I was
in for. Pedant, bigot, Salvation Army lassie—all the
familiar abuse flowed over my head. I myself had
quite a command of invective. The bullying was by
no means all on one side.

I could survive the anger of a friend of my own
generation. What hurt much more was the sadness of
some of the older people inside the Labour Party to
whom I was deeply attached. Why did I do such a
thing? Did I know what I was letting myself in for?
What hope was there of any progress at all if socialist
fought socialist? The Labour Party like every other
party had its undesirable elements. Some of its leaders
were not much use. But its rank and file? Where
could you find such people? Loyal, uncomplaining,
hard-working, selfless? Were they not worth sticking
by?

I listened, impressed up to a point, but at the back
of my mind struggling unsuccessfully to find words
that would clarify what I felt about "the splendid
rank and file" argument. I did not deny it existed. I
had no wish to deny it. I knew it to be true. But the
structure of the party was such that at critical moments
the will of the rank and file seemed never to prevail.
I felt about the majority of ordinary people inside the
Labour Party, as I feel about the great majority of
people inside Germany to-day. Who in his senses

would deny that the average German means well, loves children, loves homely worth-while things, has a right to be proud of the contribution that Germans have made to music, to literature, to philosophy, to the sciences. One could write a whole book about the virtues of the Germans. Lots of people have. But that does not alter the fact that Germany is a police state; that its people are not free; that individual judgment has been trampled underfoot; that whenever Hitler decides to embark on war, the will of the ordinary splendid rank and file Germans simply does not count. Only that of the Führer and the small clique with whom he surrounds himself.

In 1932 I was sadly, reluctantly driven to the conclusion that there was no real democracy inside the Labour Party, that the personal ascendancy of Ramsay MacDonald had been replaced by the cash plus voting power ascendancy of a trade union junta headed by Sir Walter Citrine and Mr. Ernest Bevin. The latter were no more to my liking than the former.

I had no choice but to remain with the I.L.P. I was by no means happy about my decision. I had no lack of personal friends inside the Labour Party who went to great pains to point out the unpleasant personal consequences that were bound to follow. That sent me off in search of reasons that might justify me staying with the larger organization. But the more I compared the structure, policy, programme and recent record of the two parties, the more convinced I became that my place was with the I.L.P.

183

And, of course, I hoped and trusted the British working-class movement would one day fulfil the promise of its early pioneer years. I looked eagerly both towards the I.L.P. and to the left wing inside the Labour Party to justify my hopes. One day, I told myself, these two streams would meet again!

CHAPTER XI

POLITICS, in the sense I use the word, continued to take up most of my time and energies. But I managed to sprawl around in a good number of other directions as well.

For one thing my home people wanted me to do something about the law degree I had collected in my student days. Someone put the idea into their heads that I ought to read for the Bar. In their own modest, unclamorous way they rather fancied the idea of seeing me strutting around in a curly grey wig. I don't think I took the proposition seriously for a single moment. There always seemed to me a Gilbert and Sullivan element in the whole thing. I took my politics seriously. Very little else. But I was at a loose end. I was no longer a Member of the House of Commons. And I had seen so many people let their minds go to seed by abandoning themselves exclusively to the making of propaganda speeches, that I wanted some balancing interests. Anyhow, for all sorts of reasons, muddled and otherwise, I got as far as becoming a member of Middle Temple and eating my way through a number of the ceremonial dinners that are part of the ritual that all intending barristers must observe.

A note arrived from Lord Sankey, then Lord Chancellor, inviting me to have tea with him in the House of Lords. There was nothing "official" about his invitation. It was entirely a private matter.

I do not approve of Lord Sankey—not since he followed MacDonald into the National Government—but I have a great liking for him. The name Sankey means a lot to colliers. It is associated with the most hopeful period in our history. Bob Smillie giving evidence before the Sankey Commission; Lord Sankey, then Sir John, presiding over the Commission and making no bones about his warm sympathy and concern for miners. Because of those memories, when first I came to London and was introduced to Sankey, I beamed goodwill—and he beamed back.

The next time I met him I had a young worker from a colliery village in Lanarkshire with me who had travelled four hundred and forty miles to see London and visit the House of Commons. It takes a lot of money to travel so far. I could guess what the saving of that money had meant. I was anxious to give him as good a time as I could. When we had had the inevitable tea on the Terrace and seen all that was to be seen in and around the Houses of Parliament, we walked along the embankment in the direction of the gardens that adjoin the House of Lords. I saw the Lord Chancellor approaching and told the young fellow who he was. I could see the eager interest with which he looked in Sankey's direction for, like me, he had grown up in a mining village at a time when the name

186

Sankey was on everybody's lips. This was history walk-ing towards him. When Lord Sankey passed I grabbed hold of him and introduced the two. And I was grateful to the Chancellor for the gentle, unaffected courtesy with which he helped me entertain my guest. We walked on into the gardens together, talking lightly of this and that: the Thames, the fine weather, politics, colliers. My young lad's visit to London was now quite complete.

A year later MacDonald formed the National Government. Sankey stayed with MacDonald. The Parliamentary Labour Party was summoned to Transport House to consider what next. Who would now lead the Party? What policy should be pursued? MacDonald, of course, did not attend that meeting. But Sankey was more man than that. He turned up and asked to be allowed to explain what he thought of the situation and why he had felt it his duty to go with MacDonald. At the end of his statement he put his hand on the shoulder of Arthur Henderson who was sitting on the platform beside him, and pronounced an all-inclusive benediction. MacDonald had saved the country. Arthur Henderson had saved the soul of the Labour Party. Good luck to both!

What could you make of it? Only a man of very fine personal integrity could have got off with a statement like that, to such an audience, at such a time. I decided the only thing to do was to laugh. This was "Alice in Wonderland" politics. Lord Sankey had plainly wandered in and out of the Labour Movement with only the faintest notions as to what it was all about.

I had time to recall those things on the afternoon some time later when I went to have tea with him, for when I arrived, the House was still sitting. The Lord Chancellor was still on his woolsack. I wandered around a bit then was shown to his retiring-room. A few minutes later he came sailing along in his enormous robes. We talked for a few minutes then while, at his request, I rang for tea, he disappeared into his dressing-room to disrobe. It did not take long. Almost immediately he smilingly reappeared. I felt I was playing at charades. He looked as if he felt a bit like that too.

Well, how did I like Middle Temple? It was his own particular Inn and he was much attached to it. I enlarged on a grievance that was annoying me at the time. Why could I not be permitted when I dined in the hall of the Inn, as the law obliged me to do if I wanted to be called to the Bar, to sit at table with any students or barristers present I happened to know? Why the atmosphere of a Victorian boarding-school? Why a special table isolating women students? What sort of fraternity was this that parcelled us out into separate groups according to sex, then subdivided the men according to colour? Nice memory for Indians and Africans to take back with them of their "mother" country! Unless they were fools or had no personal dignity, they were entitled bitterly to resent such segregation. It was the element of compulsion that was all wrong. Left to themselves, coloured men might prefer to dine with coloured men. Women might prefer to cluster together at the one table. But to be compelled to do it? What a silly, belittling arrangement.

Sankey listened and nodded sympathetically. Yes, but the Middle Temple was a very conservative institution. Its customs were centuries old, hallowed by time. To attempt to amend them in any way raised terrific prejudice. But he would see. He would consult his colleagues.

The rules governing dining in hall were slightly amended. But not the spirit of the place. Rather belatedly I started taking stock of what I was up against. The prejudice against women barristers in English law courts is colossal. To make even a modest beginning you must have exceptional ability, an independent income to keep you going for an indefinite number of years and a willingness to give your time and energies exclusively to furthering your professional interests. Even then it is a big gamble.

I decided I had made a mistake. I had none of the qualifications. I ought never to have begun. Above all, I was too much preoccupied with outside happenings. Other activities seemed to me much more urgent and worth-while. And so the attempt to get myself settled into a safe, respectable groove, entirely failed.

For the next five years I lived the life of a glorified hobo. At least sometimes glorified, sometimes just plain hobo. Every January I crossed to America and remained there until Easter, singing for my supper from place to place.

Looking back, I can now see that America influenced my way of looking at things, much more than I suspected at the time. In Britain for ten months of the year I was politically a partisan, feverishly, bigotedly partisan. In America, for about two months of the year, I found myself an onlooker, a reporter. A reporter hired by socialist, radical, or at least internationally-minded organizations and presenting European affairs from the standpoint of my own philosophy, but, nevertheless, a reporter. That makes a difference. I had somehow to fix all sorts of new experiences into my preconceived notions of things.

In thinking of America I jumble up memories of 1932, '33, '34, '35, and '37. Punctilious people will tell you that is very wrong. And, of course, each year showed changes. Hoover vanished, Roosevelt filled the sky. Depression gave place to mad elation and then to doubts, disappointments and then again to a feeling that anyone else in the White House might have been worse.

I watched John L. Lewis come stalking forward, his new industrial unionism laying out both the old craft unions and some of the most powerful and reactionary of America's big business monopolies. Roosevelt is obviously batting on Lewis's side and all that may one day add up to the beginnings of a genuinely new economic deal for that third of all Americans who, to quote Roosevelt himself, are underfed, under-clothed and under-housed. But, personally, I don't know. I am not competent to judge. The only thing I can be sure of is that in the American trade unions, in political groups of bewilderingly many and muddled kinds, in colleges, in some of the churches too, there is a staunch core of good Americans doing essentially the sort of things that I, too, want to have done.

But America's tragedy, like our own, is that its various socialist, communist and radical groups hate one another more than they hate any common enemy.

That is the sort of muddle that every nation not yet entirely totalitarian has got itself into. We don't seem even to have begun to understand the only means by which the democratic method can be made to work. Much that I saw and heard in America impressed on me, perhaps more vividly than might have been the case if I had never left Scotland, that if it is unanimity, regimentation we want, then we shall get it—but it will be under a fascist reign of terror. We shall have our opinionated heads knocked together and be taught to agree—the agreement of the grave. Liberty gone, dignity pilloried, the power to make individual judgments stripped from our fretful hands, the Minimum Man in the saddle, uniform and killing tackle all complete.

Learning how to agree to differ is a very hard lesson. But so is learning how to build a bridge, install radio, make a well-fitting suit of clothes. So are most of the jobs that a highly complicated modern society expects us to do. And we do them. We train to do them, often demanding of ourselves long study and a great deal of self-discipline before we are at all pleased with our workmanship. But in political matters, in the most important key job of all, we think it all right to barge forward guided only by prejudice, a few general assumptions, hates and ideals. Then collisions occur and we are angry and hurt. That sort of level of behaviour and skill on the part of motorists on American or British highways would mow down a million road users in no time.

Every spring when I returned from America I brought back the same hope. Faint, but never entirely extinguished. I was longing to be free to spend my energies clearly and extravertly fighting the social system that keeps working people weak and poor. And even at its best, even when it gives them work and bread, brands them with inferior status and torments them with uncertainty about the future.

Instead, I had to turn to with as much relish as I could muster and take part in the never-ending warfare between rival labour, communist and socialist organizations.

I regarded a great deal of that warfare as a criminal waste of energy. Disagreements, of course, there had to be. That was in the very nature of things. But I was deeply shocked and antagonized by the barbaric level at which a great deal of the controversy took place.

In Scotland, whether it is politics or theology we are quarrelling about, we are good haters. And we each

and all go into battle armed with a self-righteousness
that sometimes staggers people of a more easy-going
disposition. Each Easter when I returned from America
I felt with increasing keenness that the general political
knock-about I was expected to take part in was almost
as primitive in its nature as the behaviour of our
eighteenth-century kirk elders who upheld their
theology by burning old women suspected of witchcraft.

What worried me most was that all the time a near-
fascist National Government went on ruling Great
Britain, and looked like continuing to do so indefinitely
unless a drastically different mood could be brought
into the working-class movement. I believed it should
be possible for sincere differences of opinion between
Labour Party, Independent Labour Party and Communist Party to be stated without the controversialists
becoming mortal enemies. I believed it honourable
when those differences became acute that separate
organizations should exist side by side and each of us
choose the party with which we had most in common.
I insisted, above all, that on agreed issues and for
specific purposes, alliances ought always to be possible.
There were many people in all three parties who felt
as I did. There were also elements in all three parties
who believed in a war of mutual extermination. It was
the latter who gained the upper hand.

In November 1935 the National Government went
to the country. I was once again I.L.P. candidate in
North Lanark. All through the campaign came the
cry, sometimes wistfully, sometimes angrily, from rank

o   193

and file workers for working-class unity. Left to ourselves we might have been able to answer the cry. But the official policy of the Labour Party forbade. And quite a number of key-people inside the I.L.P. agreed with the Labour Party in this respect. The zealots in both camps wanted a war of extermination. They got it. When the votes were counted the Conservatives had won with 22,301. I followed with 17,267. The Labour Party nominee had 6,763.

And all this against a background of world events that was becoming more and more macabre. We looked on, as, with awesome momentum, calamity after calamity befell the workers of first one country and then another. First came the news that Hitler was reducing to pulp the great mass movements of the German working class. Socialist, communist, liberal parties, Jewish minorities, Catholic minorities, the Lutheran Church, all in turn were being flayed by the fascist whip.

Throughout Britain, we dimly took note of these things, regretting it all, but each warring faction rendered impotent by its exclusiveness. We were each the Lord's anointed, so could not unite with the other. Though the whole world should crash about our heads yet would we give no quarter to those who were our natural and only possible allies.

Then from Austria came desperate appeals for aid. Our beautiful Vienna and its socialist administration and all the tender, careful work that had been done there was in deadly peril.

I thought of Austria as I had first known it in the summer of 1929. The hospitable and charming household of the Scheu family. The pleasant company of newspaper men I at that time regarded as merely playboys, good companions for an occasional evening out but only remotely and trivially connected with serious socialist politics. John Gunther, large, blond and looking almost idiotically good-tempered; Frances, his wife, so tiny and dainty that I wanted to lift her up and put her on the palm of my hand. "Watch Frances, she has a jagged edge to her tongue," some acquaintances said to me. I felt very safe. It is the sickly sweet, oh, ever so sweet women who frighten me! And Gedye was there, and Bill and Tess Shirer, and Fodor (*Manchester Guardian* correspondent and a sort of father to the whole journalistic colony), and Knickerbocker breezed in and out, the most conservative of the lot in his opinions but the best dancer.

"Gedye is the pick of the bunch," young Friedl Scheu advised me. "You ought to see more of him." But I was on holiday. My standards were purely hedonistic! If I wanted to talk seriously to a newspaper man, it was Dr. Pollak I turned to, editor of the *Arbeiter-Zeitung*, Vienna's socialist daily paper.

I had a very good time in Vienna. I saw all the sights of the town—all the things that workers had built for workers. The houses and the schools and the crêches and the gay gardens and swimming-pools, finer of their kind than those in any other capital in the world.

Herbert Morrison was visiting Austria at that time

195

too, learning from Vienna how to make the parts of London where poor people live less squalid. I wish I could see more evidence that he had also learned the other lessons of Vienna. Now only a hunted illegal movement remains in our once great socialist citadel.

In Britain we were sorry when Vienna fell. Sorrier than about Germany. The Austrian workers did not run away. On every formal calculation they ought to have. They had not an earthly chance of winning. But they fought back. And for that we honoured them and felt that we ourselves had grown more wholesome. We were sorry, truly sincerely sorry when Vienna fell. But we did not see that that was any reason for pooling every scrap of strength that we could muster in a common drive against our own near-fascist Government that had helped to destroy Vienna and was preparing to destroy a good deal more. We were all so sure we were right; all so scathing about the errors of others; and all so ridiculously impotent.

Since 1929 I have watched the impact of world events cut in under the superficial cynicism of one after another of that group of foreign correspondents I then regarded as so flippantly unconcerned. *Germany Puts the Clock Back*, *Fallen Bastions*, *Disgrace Abounding*, *The Eleventh Hour*, even *Inside Europe*, all of them free from the clumsy, heavy jargon that clods the pages of most political writing. All of them readable and understandable by the ordinary people they are addressed to. All of them saying in effect, "Watch out, watch out, the barbarians are on the march. Look to

196

your defences, guard well your homes. Each man who values liberty, to his place in the ranks." The play-boys have turned evangelist. But tragic irony, many socialist leaders and some socialist rank and file too, whom I once looked to for serious sustained working-class struggle, seem to have turned playboys. They know all the language of revolt. They know all the words. They keep on repeating the old slogans over and over again. But nothing seems to invade their spirit. I refuse to believe that an informed, concerned leader-ship of the working-class movement of Great Britain could not build bridges from one sect to another, could not merge and maximize all the energies of Labour Party, Co-operative Party, I.L.P., Communist Party and not least, of that vast army of good citizens who now stand disheartened and aloof but would follow a united lead. And until something like that is done, Great Britain, God save us all, must remain at the mercy of its Chamberlains.

CHAPTER XII

SOMEWHERE in the heart of Fleet Street I have my dream editor. I have never met him but I know his voice on the telephone and, although I have failed to keep almost every other document ever sent me, affectionate, abusive, incriminating, I hold on tightly to an old letter of his. "Dear Miss Lee, Thank you very much for your article. I hope it satisfies you because it delights me. Signed, W. Midgley, *The Star*, Bouverie Street, E.C.4."

I held on tightly to that particular letter because of the time when it reached me. I had sunk into a mood of acute depression. The 1935 general election was approaching. The Labour Party had introduced a third candidate into the North Lanark constituency, thus making a Conservative victory certain. After the election I would have to decide what next I intended to do. I had come to a complete dead end. I was no use as a politician. I clung stubbornly to the proposition that the I.L.P., the Labour Party and the Communist Party, each and all professing a socialist objective, each and all having in their ranks loyal and trusting working people, should know how to come to terms with one another. But that apparently was heresy, mere senti-

198

mentality. I could find no echo of support in official quarters anywhere. So what was the use of going on? What hope was there? I hate and despise bigoted sectarianism. It is a violation of the mood and a betrayal of the hopes of rank and file members of every section of the working-class movement. I have no gift, no heart, for spending myself in that sort of warfare. One would have thought that the fate of Germany would have been a lesson to the rest of us. The German Social Democratic Party had no lack of brilliant theoreticians very, very sure of the immaculacy of their doctrines. The Communist Party of Germany was equally convinced of the perfection of its policy and tactics. But Hitler won. The ordinary people lost. And nothing it seemed could prevent the British Labour Movement from dying a similar death.

I was very weary and utterly discouraged. Here is the sort of thing that there seemed no cure for. John, Jack and Jim live in the east-end of Glasgow. John belongs to the I.L.P., Jack to the C.P., Jim to the Labour Party. They are all unemployed and line up in the same queue in the same unemployment exchange to collect their weekly "dole". Each thinks he knows everything that has happened in Russia since the Revolution, during the Revolution and before. (After Russia they were going to have Spain to quarrel about.) On the strength of listening to a speech or two, perhaps reading a pamphlet or two laying down the official "line" of their respective parties, they are for ever ready to slander and curse one another. And all the time they need only look down at the state of their boots, homewards to shabby firesides, disheartened wives, children lacking so much, so very much of even the barest necessities, to find ample and understandable territory about which to agree. Their party leaders could easily make allies of the three men. But instead they encourage them to quarrel about remote places and abstract theories regarding which they can have at most only the flimsiest second-hand knowledge. That, of course, does not make it more difficult for them to quarrel. It makes it just so much easier.

What can you do against that kind of grotesque misdirection of energy? From time to time the I.L.P. made heroic efforts to bring the various groups together. The Socialist League inside the Labour Party tried to respond but was exterminated for its pains. The Communist Party developed an ardent desire to join up with the Labour Party, but had not enough sense to realize that Labour leaders like Herbert Morrison are aware of every abusive epithet that at the same time the Communist Party keeps throwing at the I.L.P. "What kind of loving, trustworthy brother is this, that we are asked to open our doors to?" men like Morrison could well ask. And, indeed, he does.

In face of all that, I decided that there was nothing, absolutely nothing, that my own solitary self could do. Nature has its own way of carrying you through that kind of phase. Your mind and body react on one another. You become ill. The doctor calls it "a nervous breakdown". Then, somehow, as your physical self gradually repairs, your courage and hope come back too.

By the spring of 1936 I had got over my bout of depression. In particular, I was eagerly following every scrap of news that came from France. The left forces there were learning how to unite. Perhaps this was what I had been waiting for. Perhaps this was the answer to many of my questions. Perhaps France would light the way for all of us. I wanted very much to go to France to see for myself what was happening. It was then I re-read Midgley's letter and wondered if I might not try my hand at being a journalist. Why not find out whether he could use an article or two on how France was looking and behaving during its "Front Populaire" election? I decided it would be bad tactics to go the whole hog and ask him to send me to Paris. That would probably frighten him off. Instead I would telephone and say, casual like, that I was going to France anyhow, would he like an article or two? And so I did. And the perfect editor replied in the way that I had gambled on him replying. Yes, he could use two, perhaps three, descriptive articles.

That bucked me up sufficiently to approach "Reynolds". The voice at the other end of the telephone decidedly did not sound as if my offer was manna from heaven. It was a cautious Scotch voice. But all the same, I fixed up for two more articles so all I had now to do was to collect the necessary letters

of introduction to key people in the various parties of
the Left and set sail.

As a last preliminary I zig-zagged across a few
Bloomsbury Squares from my flat to where John and
Frances Gunther then lived. I went with all the
humility of a novice seeking priestly benediction; but
I was so excited that I said the wrong things. John,
usually so easy-going, looked at me almost primly.
Then he read me a lecture. Journalism was not something that any inexperienced amateur could step right
into. It was a craft, an exacting craft and needed a
long, often painful, apprenticeship. I agreed so sincerely that he relented. All right, when you get to
Paris, make straight for Edgar Mowrer, then contact
the rest of the boys. Here you are—names, addresses,
telephone numbers.

There was a very different flavour to this spring-
time election in France to the one we had muddled
through in Britain the previous autumn. I hurried
from meeting to meeting, from place to place, with
evidence everywhere that the Front Populaire, the
electoral alliance formed by socialists, communists and
liberals, was going to be a terrific success. It was a bit
strange at first getting used to seeing the tricolour and
the red flag intertwined, with socialists trying to keep
the emphasis on the red flag and communists insisting
that it be placed on the national emblem. I had always
contended that workers' organizations made a mistake
when they handed over all the emotional drive behind
patriotism and tradition to their opponents. Well, here

was an example to the contrary. How did I like it? The communists, it seemed to me, were making their usual mistake; getting on to a good idea then applying it so rigorously, so mechanically, with such false, unconvincing emphasis that they made it sound just silly. I wished they would show a little more discrimination. But why grumble? If the tactic succeeded, if the people of France elected a reliable anti-fascist, pro-workers' government, that was a good deal. It then remained to be seen if the workers could, under the wing of such a government, win solid advantages, and, having won them, keep them. What happened in France as a result of this election would have a good many lessons for the labour movements of other countries, particularly Great Britain.

The Paris election meetings I attended, whether communist, socialist or radical, were all alike. Large crowds, a loud-speaker booming over our heads, the platform party rather remote and unreal, the same old speech invariably keeping Hitler to the fore as the supreme reason why every Frenchman who loved liberty and France should vote for one or other of the "Front Populaire" candidates.

After a surfeit of large city demonstrations, I was keen to attend some village meetings where the atmosphere would be more intimate and more time allowed for "heckling".

I found exactly what I was looking for in the enormous, sprawling constituency, not unlike North Lanark, that Gaston Bergery represents. Gaston

Bergery had been described to me as a "lone wolf" type of politician, out at elbows with capitalist society but totally unable to see eye to eye with either official socialist policy or official communism. My chief interest in him was that he has been one of the first people in France to advocate an electoral alliance of all the progressive parties with the object of carrying through a programme of social reform, outwitting the growing fascist elements inside France itself and, above all, holding Hitler at bay.

I liked the whitewashed village hall where I was one of about two hundred people waiting impatiently for Bergery, the candidate, to arrive. It looked very spick and span. The dark blue shirts of the working men who sprawled about the back of the hall showed up vividly against the whiteness. So did their weather-beaten faces. They looked intelligent and aggressive. I did not like so well the people who occupied the three front rows. They were obviously the small tradesmen of the town. They wore rather shoddy conventional lounge suits and had pale, ungenerous faces. Probably all just prejudice on my part! But there you are. That is how they struck me and I had plenty of time to look at them for Bergery arrived very late. I sympathized with him. He had obviously been going from hall to hall, from village to village around a French edition of North Lanark.

When at last he arrived a group of communist workmen at the back cheered loudly and saluted him with clenched fists. I thought Bergery gave a rather

irritated look in their direction. He certainly attempted
no reciprocal fist clenching.

After he had finished speaking, quietly, conver-
sationally, persuasively, the questioning began. The
small tradesmen were on the warpath. One moved to
the front, removed his coat, draped it cloak fashion over
his shoulders, all the time gesticulating excitedly and
putting his views on the situation. And always he came
back to what was for him the key question. How could
Bergery pretend to be on the side of property and on
the side of communism at one and the same time?
Let him choose. One or the other. But not both, not
both. That could not be done.

Bergery answered competently and calmly. Then
another of the *petite bourgeoisie*, and still another, rose
to his feet and assailed him in almost the same words.
Bergery repeated his answer again and then all over
again, keeping his temper but with an increasing
effort. The gist of his reply was an appeal to the village
butcher and baker to remember that the common
enemy of France was Hitler's Germany, not Stalin's
Russia, and also to remember that the Communist
Party had come far to meet their views on property.
No one's savings would be in the least danger. Would
they not be well advised therefore to suppress antiquated prejudices, close the ranks, defeat fascism and
Vive la France!

A few days later, when all was over except the
declaration of the poll, I went to the Place de la Bastille
to listen to the loud-speakers that everywhere in the

205

streets of Paris were booming out each constituency result as soon as it became known. The people around me were mostly working-class and were dancing with joy. After that I moved on to the Café de la Paix, where the crowd looked mainly well-to-do. And there too, although less unanimously, the biggest cheers were for "Front Populaire" victories.

I was invited by a group of middle-class people, (you could fairly, I think, describe them as tepidly progressive in outlook), to join with them in toasting a communist victory that had just been blared through the air. Champagne cocktails were handed round. I said, chaffingly, were they not afraid of such a toast? Surely they had revised their opinions very considerably. "Ah, no madame, you do not understand. It is not *we* who have changed," was their smiling reply.

It was all very complicated. I had certain fears, certain reservations at the back of my mind, but I hoped it would work out all right. I hoped the ordinary people of France who were dancing in the streets with joy would not be disappointed.

That same year I found my way back to Russia. I had been there twice before. I wanted to compare notes; to see what kind of changes had taken place.

Before I left I collected a commission to write five articles for the *Daily Express*. The bargain was that I signed what I wrote and what I wrote would not in any way be censored. But I had to keep off the tread-mill as far as possible. No one wanted to hear that Russia was building factories, using tractors, abolishing illiteracy. That was not news. That had all already been said. Find new angles. Make a different approach.

Shortly before then the newspapers had carried a paragraph announcing that Schiaparelli had been to Moscow and had been invited to design model gowns for Russian women. I rapped my head against the wall and hoped I would remember that that was the sort of thing that was news. "Off you go in search of Schiaparelli," I advised myself. "Find out what she has been up to. Find out if she actually has been designing clothes for Russian women and if they are being worn and who wears them, commissar's wife or ploughman's wife."

Once in Moscow I found Schiaparelli exceedingly elusive. I could find no trace of her anywhere. No one knew anything about her. No one had heard of her. I was given a permit to attend a mannequin parade at the Dom Modelei, central fashion house for Moscow. That in itself was surely news. Mannequin show in Moscow! I go, take my seat in an elegant room, all very modern. Find factory girls, some with shawls over their heads and a peasant look, others with manicured nails, clothes and hair styles indistinguishable from those of a London shop-girl or typist, filing into the surrounding seats. The show begins. Handsome mannequins parade before us, displaying bathing and holiday garments for that trip to Odessa when summer weather comes. Afternoon gowns suitable for a quiet party or a visit to the theatre. One evening dress actually had a train to it; surely only for the very grandest of official balls!

These Russian girls enjoyed themselves enormously. Their eyes popped with pleasure each time a new exhibit was brought forward. The leading demonstrator looked at them severely and said they must not be so undiscriminating. They must consider each garment carefully and make suggestions and criticisms. I, too, was invited to criticize and promptly found myself out of favour when I sincerely did so. Lots of Russian women have short, squat figures. These types look anything but their best in jimped skirts and bodices that are an entirely uninspired imitation of the cheaper ready-made clothing you can buy in a second-rate department store in London or New York. Why not strike out on their own? I suggested. Why not beat the *bourgeoisie* fashions? I am afraid I got rather carried away with my subject. I would like to think that the interpreter who spoke for me to the girls did me less than justice. For I was rather crossly told that I was quite mistaken. The fashions I had been looking at were by Russian designers. Russia had nothing in common with *bourgeois* nations.

And still no sign of Schiaparelli. In despair I appealed to my friend, Philip Rabinovitch. He has a small, pointed face with pock markings and looks rather like Lenin. Sometimes he comes to London on trade delegations. He is a kind of cross between a junior Cabinet Minister and a big business executive. His home is a simple four-roomed affair and his wife is as competent and hard-working and charming a Bolshevik as he is. I had the pleasure of going to supper with them in their home. The great thing that evening was the photograph of a new grandchild that had just arrived. They looked at it and displayed it and loved it in that way that makes war and hatred between peoples such a foul abomination. For always in foreign countries when you get through the formalities and sit down to a family supper, you find just folks.

But I did not intend even the grandchild to side-track me from Schiaparelli. "Philip," I insisted, "you must help me. A real journalist would get to the bottom of this and here am I absolutely stumped. Get out the army, get out the Gay Pay OO, take whatever emergency measures may be necessary, but find me that Schiaparelli model!"

With an amused, tolerant gleam in the corner of his eye my friend lifted the telephone. The machinery of the State was set in motion. With mock solemnity he promised that if such a thing existed anywhere in the whole length and breadth of Russia, it would be found and I would be informed.

The following day a note arrived at my hotel along with a permit to enter the building that in Czarist times had been the Moscow Stock Exchange. I hurried along and found that one enormous room was now being used to house a sample of every kind of article that the Soviet trading authorities imported from France. It was not open to the general public. It was simply a trade show. In a humble remote corner I found Schiaparelli at last! And very nice, too! A simply-cut black dress to be worn with a matching three-

P 209

quarter length reversible coat. One side of the coat was black, the other side was bright scarlet. A perky black fish-net beret completed the outfit. So this was news. Off and tell the world! Schiaparelli rejected! Schiaparelli to be re-exported to France. Not suitable for mass reproduction, say Russian fashion experts!

Having at last tracked down Schiaparelli, I then went in search of Stalin's two youngest children. I did this with a right good will. What I would discover might or might not be "news", in a newspaper sense, but I myself was going to be supremely interested. For both of them, Svetlana, a bright little girl about ten years old, and her brother, Vassily, about five years older, were attending one of Moscow's *pukhir* high-schools. The importance of this school to me was not that it was unique—there were thousands of others exactly the same as it scattered throughout the U.S.S.R.—but that it was a sample of Russian education, 1936 model, at its most official and best.

Its competent headmaster, a distinguished Soviet pedagogue, well over sixty years of age, guided me from room to room. Each time we entered a classroom, the children rose from their desks and stood stiffly to attention. Discipline was perfect. I blinked a bit but reserved judgment.

The pride of the school was plainly its science laboratory and its workshop where model engines and aeroplanes could be made. It had a fairly good library of general literature—a group of the children told me that Dickens and Rudyard Kipling were their favourite

English authors—but the school authorities were undoubtedly placing the main emphasis on technical training.

I tried to read a wall newspaper stuck up on one of the classroom walls. The main feature of the newspaper was quite a clever caricature of a very stupid-looking little boy. What was it all about? I asked. The headmaster explained that corporal punishment was not countenanced in Russian schools but to help in maintaining discipline and, at the same time, to stimulate each child to do his or her best work, prizes were given to the most successful scholars and the children themselves dealt with particularly trying pupils, by black-listing them on the wall newspaper. Sometimes, as in the one I was looking at, tacking on a caricature.

The round of the school completed, we returned to the headmaster's private study. I had duly noted that the boy Vassily had great shaggy eyebrows like his father and that his teachers regarded him as in no way exceptional. The little girl, an attractive pretty child, was praised much more warmly. She was intelligent above the average, everyone said. But Stalin's children never even entered into the conversation that began between the headmaster and myself immediately we could settle down to talk. "What did I think of the school?" was his opening question. "Very German," I replied. That, of course, was a challenge and a criticism. I made the remark deliberately. I knew I could safely do so for the man I was talking to was no robot. Some of his friends had told me something of his background to prepare me for meeting him. In the early years of the Revolution he had been under a cloud. Krupskaya, Lenin's widow, was his friend, and helped him as much as she could. In Russia, as everywhere else, it pays to find out which way the wind is blowing and blow that way too. But in the years when Russian schools were one riotous non-stop political demonstration and every type of educational experiment, hair-brained and otherwise, was being tried out without the equipment or the trained personnel to give even good ideas the ghost of a chance, he had had too much integrity to shout hurrah and pretend that all was better than well.

Now he was back in favour. I intended, by shock tactics, if necessary, to find out if the school I had just been through represented his highest educational ideals. Without a moment's hesitation he said no, most decidedly no. But what did I suggest should be done? What would I do in his place? I knew, did I not, that throughout the U.S.S.R. there was a dangerous scarcity of skilled technicians. A modern factory, a mechanized army could not be built, equipped and made to function efficiently without trained personnel. And how long would Russia survive if its enemies abroad decided that they had no cause to fear it? I had to remember that I was not visiting a Russia surrounded by friendly neighbouring powers. The Russian worker, even the Russian schoolchild, had to pay a price for the political backwardness of countries like my own. It was we who were responsible for Russia living in constant fear of invasion. And so long as this was so, a state of emergency existed inside the Soviet Union which must inevitably colour its cultural as well as its economic life.

As he talked I thought of Walter Duranty. I first met Duranty when Frank Wise took me to dine at his Moscow flat in the summer of 1930. Throughout dinner and for a good many hours afterwards, Duranty's wisecracks and stories kept everyone greatly amused. But the recurrent refrain in all he had to say was serious and sensible: "Remember, you have come into a country that is at war. War is not pretty and not ethical. The judgments you apply to a country at war are quite different to those that fit a country that is safe and at peace."

Frank Wise was a great expert on Russian economic affairs. I had great goodwill towards the country and had read all the usual books but beyond that was a complete ignoramus.

Throughout that first visit to Russia and again in 1932, before coming to even the most tentative conclusions about much that I saw, I kept Duranty's Moscow conversations firmly in mind.

In 1932 I found a second and considerably sharper corrective against any tendency I might have had to mere querulous complaining. And I needed a corrective, for that was a famine year in parts of Russia. Very few foreigners were permitted anywhere near the famine areas. I went right through them; first the

Ukraine and then into parts of the Caucasus where there was also a good deal of hunger. At the end of it all I looked like the illustrations in Bernard Shaw's *The Adventures of The Black Girl in Her Search for God.* A hot August sun had baked me a dark brown and lack of food had made me comically angular.

The "adventure" element in that kind of journey wears thin very quickly. And the importance that food comes to have for you, has to be experienced to be realized. You reach a stage when the whole meaning of life seems to consist in getting through to somewhere where you can have white rolls and butter.

It so happens that the place I got through to was Persia. Of course, if I had lingered in Russia, once I was back on the ordinary Kutais-Tiflis-Baku route there was plenty of food to be had. It was only in certain areas that food was unobtainable.

But by going straight on to Enzeli and then to Teheran, I had the important corrective of seeing hordes of emaciated, disease-ridden beggars, weird caricatures of human beings, for whom famine was apparently a permanent condition. That was invaluable in helping me to keep my balance. The hunger, disease and illiteracy I saw tolerated in parts of Persia where British interests had dominated for centuries was an unforgettable object lesson in much that South-eastern Europe takes for granted.

I could look back to Russia with new respect. There was a war on there. And in that war, peasants who killed their live-stock and refused to cultivate the land rather than conform to Soviet methods of farming and land-holding trapped themselves into famine. It was famine from such causes that I had seen in the Ukraine. But the plus factor added by Russia was not poverty, or disease or illiteracy. It was exactly the reverse. It was the fight *against* these barbarities. And finally in Persia, I saw for the first time in my life, women walking about in what looked to me to be shapeless, black cloth coffins. Only their eyes could be seen. I was told these monstrous drapings were called *paranjas*. This was the ancient eastern way of life for women. And against all that, too, Russia was fighting a terrific, lonely and many-sided battle.

In 1930 and 1932 Walter Duranty and Persia helped me when looking at Russia to keep in mind what many people seem to forget. Not just where it was trying to go but where it had come from and the stupendous obstacles that slowed down its advance at every stage of its journey. In 1936 a Moscow schoolmaster helped me in a similar way. He said nothing I had not already heard. There was nothing dazzling or original about his arguments.

But I knew no answer to them. Russia expected any day to be drawn into war. Everything it did was necessarily conditioned by that prospect. And in spite of the burdens imposed by war preparations, the ordinary Russian worker plainly enjoyed better food, clothing, medical services, opportunities for education and entertainment than ever before in his history.

I travelled back through Europe in a much more

optimistic mood than I had been in the previous autumn. The general balance of power in the world had by no means toppled over on the side of fascism. I was quite sure that even inside Hitler's Germany there were millions of people secretly opposed to the policies of their government. Franklin Delano Roosevelt, a liberal, was America's President. Léon Blum, socialist, was at that moment Prime Minister of France. That did not mean as much as it looks, of course. I knew perfectly well that in France and America there were powerful influences at work irreconcilably profascist whatever the passing character of their government might be.

And, adding enormously to the general feeling of confusion and uncertainty, there was the problem of Great Britain's behaviour. I was anxious to be home again. Wherever I went I had been asked if British people realized the extent to which the British "National" Government was helping the fascist powers. I could honestly say "no". Was there any chance of getting rid of it? Was there any hope of a Labour Government? Or a "Front Populaire" Government? What sort of socialist movement had we in Great Britain? All these were more difficult questions to answer. But I did so as fairly as I could. When in doubt I perhaps tipped the balance over on the side of optimism. But then I felt optimistic. That was in the early summer of 1936. We had not yet betrayed Spain.

CHAPTER XIII

IN the autumn of 1936 I looked forward with a good deal of pleasure to revisiting Edinburgh. There were several good reasons for that. The most important of these was Aneurin. We had been married for more than a year. I had been trailed all around Wales, north, south, highlands and lowlands. I am not complaining about that. Indeed, I am very grateful. And the pride and careful generalship with which he presented his country to me made me chuckle under my breath for his behaviour was far from squaring with the irreverent things his tongue is for ever saying.

Now I was anxious to show him Scotland. And I had made a firm resolution not to be unchivalrous. Not to point out that the mountains of Wales are lovely, but the best of our Scottish scenery is much lovelier, the cities of Wales have their good points but not one of them can compare with Edinburgh.

Our marriage had put my mother in a very awkward political dilemma. Aneurin was Labour M.P. for Ebbw Vale. I was, of course, still a member of the I.L.P. Mother is nothing if not loyal. Until that time she had been a staunch member of the Independent

Labour Party. After our marriage she continued to be a staunch member of the I.L.P. but became a supporter of the Labour Party as well. If you want to know how she did it, you must ask mother. She has a special genius for that kind of thing.

And no amount of arguing or chaffing on our part could make her budge from her position. I had to resign myself to this very disconcerting fact. For more than four years, the I.L.P. and Labour Party had been separate, often hostile, organizations. She had attended scores of I.L.P. meetings, lived in an atmosphere of continual political discussion, heard the case put for the I.L.P. from every conceivable angle. And in spite of all that she still had not the faintest notion as to what the quarrel between the two parties was really about. For her spirit refused to listen to any of the formal arguments. It simply cried out for unity and insisted on having it.

It was quite clear that the I.L.P. could make no great headway so long as it had people like mother to grapple with. For her way of looking at things is typical of ninety-nine per cent of the men and women who, either actively or passively, take any part in Labour politics.

I had her very much in mind as I travelled up to Scotland in the autumn of 1936. The annual conference of the Labour Party was being held in Edinburgh that year. I went along to it with great goodwill. I was very anxious to see the old alliance between Labour Party and I.L.P. re-established. Aneurin was in Edinburgh attending the conference as a delegate. I was there to report for the *New Leader*. Immediately it was over we planned to begin our holiday.

But we had no holiday. We had no heart for holidaying. Not after what was done in our name at that Edinburgh conference. Perhaps you already know all about it, but in case not let me tell you, for it is a very important part of this whole history.

The main issue before conference delegates was the civil war in Spain. Right on the dot from the firing of the first shot, there seemed to me one stand and only one that any socialist could take. Uphold the right of the Spanish Government to buy arms. Spanish generals and *grandees* had barricaded themselves in behind German guns and opened fire on the working people of Spain. The Spanish Government needed arms to quell the rebellion. It tried to purchase the material it required in the usual way, as governments have always done and as every principle and precedent of international law entitles them to do. But the Spanish Government found that its way had been barred. It was not to be allowed to buy arms. The governments of France and Britain had evolved an extraordinary scheme called non-intervention. Neither Spanish insurgents nor the elected Government of Spain was to be allowed to buy arms from abroad. They were to carry on their fight strictly within the frontiers of Spain, having at their disposal only such arms as they possessed or could manufacture for themselves.

The British Government called into conference the leaders of the British Labour Party. At the annual conference of their Party those same leaders turned up with a more than usually "weighty" air. Their manner conveyed that they knew a great deal more than it was expedient to say. The conference had better take their word for it that non-intervention was in the best interests of the Spanish people, of the British people, of the cause of peace.

Isabel de Palencia, a member of the Spanish Cortes, who had been sent from Spain to explain to this working-class assembly her people's desperate need of arms, was, after a good deal of back-stair diplomacy, granted permission to speak. When she ended her appeal almost everyone in the hall was in tears. But the speech and the weeping were carefully timed. Those responsible for conference arrangements saw to it that the Spaniard was not allowed to present her case until *after* the vote had been taken that told the world British Labour had come down on the side of "non-intervention". The Spanish Government had informed us quite definitely and categorically that "non-intervention" was a farce. That the fascist powers were sending arms and men to aid the Spanish fascists.

Nevertheless, British Labour voted in support of "non-intervention". While the votes were being counted I was facing the delegates from the press table at the front of the hall and could see the cards held up. The Little Fellows, that is, the local labour parties, were doing their best. By an overwhelming majority they asked that Spanish working-men should not be denied arms. But the Big Fellows, the holders of the block trade-union votes, controlling almost five-sixths of the total votes cast at annual Labour Party conferences, decided otherwise. Up went the cards with hundreds instead of ones and twos on them, in support of "non-intervention".

When the result of the voting was announced, and again after the Spanish visitor had made her appeal, a howl of protest went up from the body of the hall. The party leaders rode the storm by promising that they would make the British Government make the German and Italian Governments carry out "non-intervention" with rigid impartiality. If the Spanish Government was denied arms they would see to it that so were the Spanish fascists. Mr. Ernest Bevin, leader of the Transport and General Workers' Union, went so far as to say that he would sit on the doorstep of 10 Downing Street and not budge until the Prime Minister had given him satisfactory assurances.

It was very silly of Mr. Bevin to talk in that way. He ought to have known better. But British Labour leaders have a monotonous willingness to trust to promises made to them by conservative politicians; and the equally monotonous aftermath is the air of hurt surprise with which they later return to tell us that we have all once again been let down.

Not many delegates in that Edinburgh conference hall got any real comfort from Mr. Bevin's speech. Very few indeed were ingenuous enough to believe that it was safe to place any reliance on promises made by Mr. Chamberlain, still less, promises made by Herr Hitler.

The dreadful reality behind all our talk was that Spanish workers were waiting on Spanish battlefields for arms with which to hold back steel-clad fascist troops. Almost all the world had taken sides against the working-people of Spain. They had hardly anyone they could look to except us. They were appealing to us to uphold their right to buy arms. And we, their natural allies, friends and supporters, were dithering and equivocating lost in a mist of words.

At the end of the proceedings delegates were called on to rise to their feet and sing the "Internationale".

"Then comrades, come rally"—that was too much. I was not supposed to have any part in conference business. Neither had I officially. I was at the press table. But I was not made of wood. I crept miserably out of the hall and stumbled into Aneurin. He looked haggard and careworn. He was ill anyhow at the time and in no condition to stand punishment. He looked as if he had just dragged himself out of a torture chamber. And he was not the only delegate who looked like that. Out they came, singly and in groups, the most unhappy, guilty-looking collection of people I have ever seen. Their very misery made me hope again. If they felt like that something perhaps could still be done.

That evening there was no need for me to ask Aneurin where his thoughts were, for mine were there too. We had been to Spain together a year before the civil war began. We went there to recover from the fuss of getting married. There was nothing at all political about that first visit to Spain. It was planned entirely as a holiday. While there we were both as nearly carefree as the circumstances of our lives had ever allowed either of us to be.

If you live most of your years in a Scottish or Welsh colliery district, then one day find yourself breakfasting out of doors in January (in January, mark you!) with orange-groves around you, the Sierra Nevada on the sky-line and a brilliant blue-green sea at your feet, you rediscover all your childhood's faith in miracles.

Aneurin, who when he is among Englishmen always seems to me an alien figure—he is much too unequivocally alive to suit staid English ways—looked utterly at home in Andalusia. He loved it all. The vivid colouring, the smell and flavour of the place, the warmth, the dark, proud-spirited people.

The fishermen and field-workers of Torre Molinos are almost all socialists or communists. Once they knew we were on their side they smiled and were friendly. It was a great lark the day Aneurin got himself a magnificent Spanish cloak, a sombrero, a scarlet facha to wind round his waist, and because we had dared him to do it, went swaggering dressed like this along the winding village street that leads down to the sea. As he passed along the older people grinned to him more broadly than usual. The young senoritas shrieked with delight. I can see them all as they were that day. I am sure those Andalusian peasants thought we were quite mad. But I am also sure they trusted us. That is why he and I have such bitter reason for shame. We made promises to those Spanish people that we failed to keep. I don't mean promises made in so many words. There was no need for that. The pledge we made was implicit in our relationship.

After what came to be called the Spanish "civil" war began, Madame Vandervelde was the first to give us news of Torre Molinos. She left shortly before it fell to the fascists. Sick with foreknowledge, I listened to what she had to say. On the day she left, a group of women gathered around her in the main street of the village crying brokenly, "Los Moros, los Moros". I could see those Spanish women; hear the dread in their voices. I had known some of them. "Los Moros". The Moors. The Moors were coming. Black troops were being rushed along the coast road. Black troops with German guns and Italian conscripts to aid them.

The men of Torre Molinos, its fishermen and field-workers were mobilizing to defend their homes armed with little more than spades and fishing-tackle.

Spades and fishing-tackle and antiquated rifles and home-made explosives against the devilish perfection of the most up-to-date armaments that the most up-to-date factories in the world could produce. That was how we left our friends to fight. The fascists of Germany and Italy kept faith with the fascists of Spain. They promised them arms and men and gave both in full measure. It was only we who failed to keep faith. It was we whose stock-in-trade for generations had been phrases such as "Workers of the world unite", who, when it came to a show-down, ratted.

It was not even as if we had been asked to do anything very heroic. The Spanish people did not ask us to send our men to fight for them. They did not even ask us to make them a present of guns. All they asked was that the voice and vote of every member of the British working-class movement should be united in demanding that the Spanish Government should not have to hold back fully-armed fascist troops with the bodies of unarmed Spanish workers.

Nine months after the Edinburgh conference, two miles from Huesca on the Aragon front, I saw for myself how non-intervention worked out in practice. Fascist troops were in possession of Huesca. Suddenly I heard what sounded like the recurrent noise of thunder in the air. I was stupidly slow to grasp what was happening. There were soldiers in Huesca, fascist soldiers who had pointed their guns in the direction of the mill-house where I was sheltering. They were concentrating on hitting the building. They knew Government troops were quartered there. I had only the vaguest notion as to what the effect of cannon-fire discharged at a range of just over two miles would be if the fascists should make a direct hit. But I had sense enough to know that that was not the moment to start trying to make any inquiries. If I could not be useful, I had better at least stand by quietly and not make a nuisance of myself. We had all been ordered to go down

Q   225

into the large basement kitchen of the mill-house. In a small side-room I could hear two telephone operators at work. Sometimes they tried a dozen times before their rapid tapping brought any response from other parts of the line. I wondered what that might mean. But my chief attention was given to young Galahad. He looked about seventeen but had told me at least half a dozen times, when I had been chaffing him, that he was twenty-two. Small, dark, vivacious, very completely a young Catalan worker. He had been told when we left Barcelona to keep beside me because of his knowledge of French. His command of the French language was about as sketchy as my own, but we managed to talk together reasonably coherently. His chief concern as we drew nearer the fighting line was that the support holding his rifle on his shoulder had snapped. It looked to me a feeble piece of string, not worth mending. I produced a leather belt that I had wound around my attache-case and offered it to him. That made us indissoluble friends. The old support for his rifle was thrown away and my bright new British belt took its place.

I watched him standing in the mill-house kitchen while the fascist guns barked around us, alert for whatever might happen. He stood at an opening that had once been a window, looking in the Huesca direction. Several times he turned his head to look back to see how I was taking it all, each time tapping the belt on his shoulder and grinning as if to say, "Leave it to us. My belt and I will hold them back!"

I know nothing about military matters. I barely know the difference between one end of a rifle and the other end. But a child could have told that these youngsters with their antiquated guns, their improvised quarters and their eager air, had not yet seen any real fighting and would go down like chaff before efficiently-trained and armed soldiery.

That, in fact, was what happened later in the war when the fighting began in earnest on the Aragon front. There is a great deal more to that Aragon story beside lack of arms. A tortuous and terrible tale of sectarian fighting behind the lines that may some day be fully and fairly told. But I am not qualified to tell it. Nor was it the decisive factor that enabled General Franco to march through Barcelona. He got there primarily because the Spanish people were starved of arms. I saw that side of things with my own eyes. I listened to groups of soldiers in place after place along the Aragon front demanding arms with which to consolidate the ground they held and prepare a great offensive. I listened to a Spanish officer addressing group after group of Catalan soldiers in these terms: They must be patient. They must trust. There were not enough arms to meet the needs on all the fronts. The main brunt of the fighting was in the Madrid sector. Arms had had to be concentrated where the enemy offensive was heaviest——

Back in Barcelona I called at the head offices of the C.N.T., the mass trade union of the workers of Catalonia, to ask advice regarding what should be said to young men in Britain who were beginning to offer themselves as volunteers for Spain.

The union official I talked with took me to the window of his office and pointed to the street below. A steady stream of young men in civilian clothes were promenading up and down. "We are not short of men," he muttered, with an undercurrent of anger and hostility in his tone. "Particularly we don't want foreigners coming here to tell us how to conduct Spanish affairs. What we need is guns. Look here," going to his desk and taking out a handful of cartridges, "we don't even have enough of these to feed the rifles already in use. Send guns. Break down the embargo on arms. That is how those of you in other countries who feel well disposed towards us can best help us win. If you send the guns, we will do the fighting. Spaniards don't want to look on while foreigners do their fighting for them."

Access to arms. That was the essential thing.

The evening before I returned from Barcelona I bought a huge slab of marzipan. I bought it for young Bob Smillie. That was in the first year of the war before the food situation had become acute. The marzipan, I was told, was Catalan Christmas cake. I knew Bob was very fond of it and I had noticed that the food he was having in the very spartan hotel where he was quartered, although at that time adequate, was exceedingly stodgy and monotonous.

I had arranged to have a farewell cup of coffee with him in one of the cafés about nine in the evening. I had business to attend to that kept me occupied until nearly midnight. So, by the time I reached the café, Bob had decided I had forgotten about him and had gone off to bed. John McNair, who had been with me all evening, took me to the room that he and young Smillie shared. A tousled mop of straw-coloured hair appeared above the bedclothes. Bob was at once eager to get up and begin the evening all over again. There was a photograph of a very young woman on the small table beside his bed. I asked him who his "girl" was. He grinned and refused to tell. "Was she Spanish?" At that he nodded in a way that plainly meant "No". "Was she Scotch?" This time he smiled happily in a way that very evidently meant that my second guess was a success.

I offered to look out of the window and whistle while he jumped into his clothes. He was up like a shot. We all three went out together.

About one o'clock in the morning, John McNair shook a middle-aged head and advised young Smillie to leave the marzipan until the next day. But Bob was at the sweet-tooth age. And I had by no means passed it. So we dined handsomely on coffee and cake.

I was very attached to this grandson of another great Bob Smillie. I had not known him at all intimately for long. But that was not necessary. There were no layers of guile or deception to be got through in order to know him. I was thankful he had not a penny-in-a-slot machine kind of mind with a ready-made answer waiting to pop out in reply to every question under the sun.

He did not pretend that he knew the answer to everything. He had much too good a mind for that. He was fumbling his way with utter integrity towards his own verities.

He was obviously a great favourite with everyone around him. He was speaking French competently and making good progress with his Spanish. And he was following with an acute and unprejudiced mind not just the broad issues of the fight between the fascists and the government forces, but the infinitely wearing and complex polemics going on among the various socialist, communist and anarchist groups. I liked above all the generosity of his temperament and judgments.

Scotland is well supplied with socialists puritanical and parochial in outlook to a degree that stultifies a good deal of their usefulness. Bob's mind and experiences were outgrowing the swaddling clothes of his early environment. But that did not mean that he was losing any of his passionate sincerity, his incorruptible devotion to the service of the poor.

When the military situation in Spain became more critical, he was one of the army of young men who, (we having failed to send arms) tried to make amends by offering their bodies. He had been in the firing-line but was recalled to Great Britain to help the Independent Labour Party explain to the British public what the real situation and needs of the Spanish people were. He got no further than the frontier. He was detained there and died of appendicitis. An illness of that kind would have been a trifling matter if he had been in

Scotland. It would have kept him in bed for a few weeks. It would not have killed him. He died for the Spanish people just as surely as if a bullet had been put through his heart in a front-line trench.

And he was just one of many. I do not add a catalogue of names. That would be too paltry, too mechanical a tribute.

In time the British Labour Party came to see that "non-intervention" did not mean what Mr. Chamberlain had assured them it would mean. In a perfunctory kind of way it declared in favour of the right of the Spanish Government to buy arms.

We all redoubled our efforts to send food and medical aid to Spain. But on the larger and decisive issue of arms, nothing was done; very little was even attempted.

The Spanish Government, no doubt biting back the bitter words that could easily have come to its tongue, said thank you to us very nicely for the food and bandages we sent. The fascists of Spain had more substantial cause for thanking their friends in other countries. Even the very best type of British bandage is not much use against a German gun. The fascists won the war.

CHAPTER XIV

AFTER Edinburgh I went home to Fife. Over the Forth as I had done so often before, back to home-people and home-places, back to a colliery district where very few people give themselves fake fancy airs and graces and where you have more chance of hearing people say what they really have in their minds, in simple forthright language, too, than anywhere else I know.

First I wanted a long sleep. Our mother is very good about sleep. It is the best kind of medicine, she maintains. You can be quite sure she will leave you undisturbed for what she calls a good round of the clock and when at last you wake all your clothes will be washed and pressed, you will know the beatitude of finding a pair of stockings waiting for you miraculously free from ladders, but you will be lucky if you can find a pair of shoes to put on. A little patience, though, and your shoes will be back from the cobbler's and you will promise for the hundredth time in your life that you will never again let yourself get so far down at the heel.

This time I had come back to make Lochgelly the starting-point in a long pilgrimage. Not so long,

measured in geographical miles, as many of the
journeys I had made already, across Europe, down
through Russia, zig-zagging in a kind of stagger dance
from one lecture engagement to another up and down,
out and about, and around the whole of the U.S.A.
But much more important than any of these others.
At least much more important for me. I was set on
exploring right into the heart of my own discontents.
I felt I could hardly bear to go on living unless I could
get to the bottom of a mystery that was poisoning the
whole of life for me. Why was Aneurin so often sad
now? Why did my father sit by the fire gently cynical
about the whole socialist movement that had once
been for him ground so sacred that he taught us to
tread reverently whenever we approached it? Why
were all the finest people I knew in the grip of a kind
of spiritual paralysis? Where was all the vigour, the
belligerency, the robust certainties that had characterized the Labour movement as I remembered it in
my teens and early twenties? Or was I merely the
victim of a very ordinary piece of self-delusion? Was
it merely my own age and circumstances that were
changing, making me raise a querulous voice, the sort
of voice that has been heard from the beginning of
time, to complain, "Ah, it was not like that in *my*
young days." I did not feel as old as all that. But I had
better be careful! I was in my early thirties. Not old,
but certainly not a child any longer.

I decided I would begin my quest by strolling
through the town, talking less and listening more than

I was in the habit of doing. I wanted to know what
people were thinking about some of the decisions the
Labour Party conference had just reached. I wanted
to know what was in their minds regarding the whole
gamut of current affairs. I knew that if I had lost my
way, got badly out of step, I would very soon be told
about it.

At the corner of the street I met John ——, collier.
His brother-in-law, the dust-cart man, joined us a few
minutes later, and, before I got home again, I had run
into Jack ——, joiner, Joe ——, butcher, and half a
dozen others as well. None of them seemed to have any
enthusiasm about any of the sort of things I wanted
them to talk about. Minds flicked off as quickly as
possible to the football team, the weekly pool, the
weather. To all sorts of inconsequential things. Politics
was very much a back number.

All those men voted Labour in the Parliamentary
elections. But voted with an indifferent shrug of the
shoulders. What else was there to vote for? Tories and
Liberals were no use to a working-man. All those men
had lived through phases of intense social and politicial
concern. More than once they had thought that
Jerusalem was just around the corner. They had grown
jaded with so many emotional ups and downs. Now
they seemed to be settling down to a grey twilight of
indifference. They could no longer be searingly disappointed. For they no longer hoped for much.
Politics? It was all a game—everyone out for himself.
You are a fool, Jennie. A fool for yourself. You ought

to get back inside the Labour Party. And, anyhow, splits are no good. No good to anybody. You can't expect to get anywhere with the I.L.P., the Labour Party, and the Communist Party all at one another's throats. People don't know which of you to believe. It is about time you all learned to agree among yourselves. You might have a chance then.

I got the talk round to Spain. You know what's the matter, don't you, says John ——, collier, with a grin one remove from a sneer. The Labour Party is afraid of the Catholic vote. Honest to God, some of them would sooner see the whole of Spain go up in smoke than damage their election chances. That's what is at the bottom of it. So-an'-So is lying low. He is trying to wangle so as to please everybody. I tell you it's a scream watching some of their antics.

I trailed home, not feeling very encouraged and wondering just what it would take to bring back the old clean fire. I knew it could be done, but what would it take to do it? Would anything short of dynamite be able to pierce through so many years of dwindling hopes?

In our house, supper is anybody's meal who likes to drop in. Sandy Brown called to see about some I.L.P. business. Sandy is one of my heroes. You could boil him in vinegar for a hundred years and still not make him sour. I have a small brown jug he sent me as a wedding present standing on a ledge above my desk. I had admired it once—it has real beauty—when I looked in to see him in his tiny single-roomed cottage

235

where he keeps house for himself, managing somehow on his ten shillings old-age pension, a shilling or two extra from the P.A.C., another shilling or two from his garden, total from all sources, well under £1 a week.

I remember his present arriving at my bright new London flat. Beneath the brown paper on the outside of the parcel there were layers of newspapers then the jug itself carefully wrapped in some of Sandy's old pit socks that had been darned and darned and crept in with the wash until it was a problem figuring out what in the world it was he had got hold of as packing. The plump little warm brown jug looked rather like Sandy himself. It was not in the least put out by its rather uppish modern surroundings, but settled down with such a friendly look, such good-tempered self-possession, that I decided whatever else might have to be displaced, Sandy had arrived to stay.

But what I started to tell you about was that other evening when Sandy dropped in in time for supper. He had on a new pair of trousers. At least somebody's old trousers made down to fit him. Sandy is short in the leg. "What do you think of them," he demanded, and it was plain from the twinkle in his eye that he had something more to say. "You look a toff," we replied. "What do you think yourself?" "Ah, weel," says Sandy, "they are a' recht, only ye ken, when I want to put my hands in ma pockets, I declare to God I hae to gang doon on ma bended knees." Sandy enjoyed his joke. So did we all. And it would have been quite out-of-place for me to have broken into the chaffing with a

236

dull harangue explaining what another part of my mind was thinking.

But I did not really enjoy seeing my old friend going around in these made-down trousers. It was not just the trousers, it was the whole pack of values they symbolized. Sandy had had to work, as all colliers have, very hard for his living. He had gone on working until he was too old to be needed any longer by the pits. And now, here he was thrown on the scrap-heap; left to make do with a ten-shilling old-age pension and "pickings" such as the cast-off clothing of some other man who had probably not worked half as hard as himself, if he had worked at all. Probably some other man who thought he was behaving with the utmost Christian charity in thus helping his poorer brethren.

Ugh! I hate the stench that rises from the word charity. The well-oiled conscience of the well-to-do, or the relatively well-to-do, satisfied to see working-people harassed and humbled by poverty, hostile to every honest-to-God effort to root out the causes of poverty, but at hand to plaster over the worst of the wounds that they themselves have helped to inflict, with a nice warm blanket for the children's bed, Mrs. Jones, a packet of tea for grandma, Mrs. Brown, would you like me to send down my last winter's coat, Mrs. Murphy? You can turn it and make quite a grand school dress for Mary Jane.

One of the snags when you try to settle down for a quiet evening under my mother's roof is the number of times people come knocking at the back door. Particularly on Thursday night. Out she goes to the kitchen, you hear a slight scuffling and whispering then back she comes trying to look as if there had been no one there. If you ask her she may tell you who it was, or, more likely, she will say, "Never mind. Poor folks don't like to be affronted with everybody knowing their way of doing."

By Thursday evening last week's pay has dwindled to nothing, if it has survived till then, and it is not everybody whose credit is good enough to tide them over until pay-day comes again. And if you have no money, no credit, young mouths to feed, what can you do? Smother your pride and try to think which of your neighbours is kindly enough, and at the same time able, to lend you a loaf, a store "check", a shilling or half a crown on the strict promise that it will be repaid in two days' time.

Almost any neighbour could knock at any other neighbour's door in our mining villages and ask help and be given it, if it was only a matter of finding someone kindly disposed. But when you put on your old coat and the grey felt hat you bought at a clearance sale the year before the flood and go out to borrow a shilling it is not such an easy matter as all that. For you have to find someone who besides being well disposed, is not in quite as desperate a plight as yourself. Mother had all the qualifications—feeling-hearted, discreet, just a little bit above the hunger line.

She did a thriving business. Thursday night, "Please could I have a little obligement, Mrs. Lee?" Saturday

night, "Here you are, Mrs. Lee, and thank you very
much. I'm very much obliged!" Sometimes, when I
questioned her about these very private transactions,
she would look at me distrustfully and shy away.
What did I want to know for? But if I persisted she
would first threaten me with what she would do to me
if I should as much as breathe a word to a single soul of
anything she said. Then she would talk. Talk soberly
and tenderly, first of this one, then of the next. How
could Martha be expected to manage with only one
man's pay among so many of them? And they were
the unlucky ones, too. Always some little accident.
Nothing serious, but enough to keep putting them back
just whenever they thought they were getting their
heads above water. Bessie used to think it would be
easier on her once her family was up a bit and started
to work. But now she is learning her mistake. It would
take a fortune, she said to me, to keep them going.
Puir young things! The things they want are innocent
enough. It would be unnatural at their age if they were
not for ever wanting. But it is hard on Bessie. She tries
to do too much and just lands herself in a hole.

Did I know that Jean's laddie had got a start? That
would give them a lift. And not before time. She has
hungered herself for those bairns. I was thankful to
see her out at the whist drive the other night. Take
her mind off her troubles for a little bit. That's right,
Jean, I said to her. You start looking after yourself
for a change. You'll be all the more thought of.

Once started on this kind of monologue, mother can

go on for ever. Not sitting down to talk—it would never occur to her that talking in itself could be an occupation —but keeping on at the same time with whatever household task she happens to be doing, sometimes disappearing into the kitchen for quite a time then re-emerging to ask if I remembered So-and-So, and did I know——

I don't often go visiting in Lochgelly. I don't have to. I can sit by our own fireside and know all that is going on. Friends and neighbours keep coming out and in, bringing their news and their views with them.

But when I heard that Mrs. Foote had been ill, that was a different matter. I must go and see her. And ex-Provost Foote, too. I was feeling restless. I was looking for something. These two were part of the legend, of the story that had started me off on all my escapades. They were old socialists. I would find a book-case in their parlour containing the same mixture of standard classics and socialist literature as in my father's bookcase. Our two families had been friends for three generations; since the time when my grand-father, an orphan of twelve, brought over from the Lothians by his uncle, first saw a coal-pit. Both families were colliers, scholars, socialists of long standing. There had never been a time when they had not rebelled against the raw, racking poverty and labour of a miner's life.

The struggle to build a union, a Co-operative move-ment, a socialist party; the eager reading of books and pamphlets and the weekly socialist Press. The punishment and distresses that are thrown on people whose views are in advance of the majority; the feeling of growth, of future greatness, of the society that is to be that keeps you going through all the darkness. Old Mrs. Foote can tell you more of the inwardness of such things than ever you will find in books.

When I walked down through the town and knocked at her trim cottage door, it was past teatime. But we started tea all over again. If you know Scotland at all, you know that the freshly-made pot of tea has very little to do with the needs of the stomach. It is a symbol, a ritual, a sacrament. You are a friend. You are being made to feel welcome. And there is nothing in the world more pleasant than such homely, sincere hospitality.

We talked until the darkness closed round the fireside and the curtains had to be drawn and the lamps lit. New-fangled electric-lamps, bright and clean, much less work for the housewife than the old-fashioned paraffin oil.

But there was no electric light in the Lochgelly our minds had travelled to. We had wandered back through the years. Back much further than my memories, back to when they themselves were just children. "Yes," said Mrs. Foote, "I can remember my father coming in and saying to my mother, 'How many bowls of porridge Tib can you make from a peck of meal? Don't lose heart, lass. Don't lose heart. If you can spin it out, we will beat them yet.'"

She is telling us about 1870 and '71. The Fife

miners are fighting for the eight hours' working-day.
I forget the present. I have gone back more than sixty
years. I am a collier hewing coal in a narrow underground seam and every little while peering out
anxiously to see if the hutches[1] are arriving. None
come. I curse and understand quite well what is
happening. The coal company is out for murder again.
Out to break me or starve me. No hutches. The swine.
No hutches, so no wages and hunger enough at home
already. Just before finishing time the hutches come
hurtling through. I load them like a man gone mad.
It is bread I am shovelling not coal. Bread to take home,
bread for the wife and for the bairns. For John and Jean
and Tam and all the rest of them. It will soon be two
o'clock. I must stop then, dead to the minute. Not a
shovelful, not so much as a single pebble of coal after
two o'clock. I promised that. I pledged myself to my
workmates. None of us to work a minute longer than
eight hours. I must keep my word. I must not have
eyes look at me accusingly and folks spit at the mention
of my name. I must stand true. What other hope is
there? Last winter I scarcely saw the light of day.
Up in the dark morning, the bairns still all in bed.
Home in the dark evening, the bairns already sleeping.
Soon they'll hardly know their daddy. What a life for a
man! No life at all. Just slavery.

But patience, thole a bit longer, and we will win yet!

[1] Hutches or "trams" are small trucks for carrying the coal to
the surface of the pit and the miner's wage is reckoned only after
the coal is taken to the surface, weighed and checked.

Alexander Macdonald said we could. He had a grand turnout to his meeting on the Birnae Braes. Hold together, men, he said, hold together and you will win. You will establish an eight hours' working-day for the miners of Fife and be the first in all the land to do so. Aye, but who would have thought the Company would hold back the hutches so that a man could get no coal carried away and that then, like the devil himself, they would tempt tired, penniless men by sending in the hutches as fast as they could follow one another, in the last hour of the shift. It's plain what they are after. Tempting us; tempting us to betray one another. To go on working long past the eight hours. And if we do, what then? Nothing to look forward to but the life of a pit rat, starvation wages, never seeing the light of day, not so much as a single hour when we can look up at the sun and call our souls our own. We must stick it no matter what it costs. But at two o'clock I must not think of the wife or I may weaken. Poor girl, it is a hard life for her. Harder, maybe, than for me. She can't work miracles. She can't feed us if there is no money to feed us with. I must get her to come out to the meetings. She would understand better then what it is all about. She is shy about coming out, prideful, woman-like, not wanting to be affronted showing everybody her old patched clothes. As if others were not as badly off as herself. And what can a man do? The Company has the pull. It has the money and the power. There is only one thing we have; just one weapon in our hands. We can hold together, keep our plighted word, not give in, stick whatever suffering may be entailed until the Company learns we are men, not beasts, and that our union is something they will have to reckon with, have to learn to respect.

And so, racked with anger, sorrow and labour, the miners of Fife in 1870 and '71 and '72 held out for the eight hours' day. They won. The Franco-Prussian war helped them to win. Coal prices soared. The coal companies saw their chance of quick, easy profits. But for that they needed the co-operation of the men. The men said they could have it—on terms. The eight-hour working day.

The years pass. It is 1894. I am my grandfather sitting by the roadside wondering where next I can turn. I have been a ringleader in a recent strike. The men are back at work, but no colliery will employ me. My friend, Jock Simpson, passes by. "Where are you off to, Jock? To the Mary Pit? No use. There are no openings there. I have just been inquiring!" Jock tells me to sit where I am till he comes back. He goes to the Mary, fixes up a job for himself and a neighbour and comes back gleefully to tell me. I am to start work with him the following day. I hurry home with my news. We are uplifted and much relieved. One of the bairns goes round to Tam Dicks for a pennyworth of pease meal. There is some churn-milk in the press. We can make brose and survive somehow until pay-day.

The next morning I rise at dawn and get into my working clothes, thankful, very thankful that the weeks of drudging from pit to pit in search of work are over.

But when I reach the "Mary" the oversman meets me and asks where I am going. "No, Michael, you are not wanted here. I did not know it was you Jock was bringing as a neighbour. Sorry, Mick, I'm very sorry, but these are my orders. It is not in my power to let you start!" And so sadly home again. The men have been at work three weeks. I have tried everywhere. The bar is up. Managers have their orders. I am not to be employed. The whole world looks black. No hope, no help anywhere. And then comes the news that causes that great lifting of the heart. The men have heard what is happening. They are angry and loyal. Strike notices are being sent round the lodges. Michael Lee must be given a start or every miner in Fife will lift his graith.

1897—the coal company thinks it can dictate even who my doctor is to be. I won't submit to that. I don't want their hand-picked nominee. I want Dr. Dandial, who lives among us, is liked and is a fine doctor. The men stand by one another once more. Every fortnight you will see them lining up outside Henderson's hall waiting to pay their union dues and their pennies for Dr. Dandial. I am a committee man sitting at the table inside the hall, collecting and counting the money, planning all the things our union will one day do as the men learn more and more the power that union gives them.

1898—I have been elected to Lochgelly Town Council.

During the campaign I say exactly what I think about slum property owners and their sinful rack-renting ways. My opponent is also my landlord. I win the election but lose my home. I, the wife and all the children are thrown out on the street. I have been evicted.

Such was my grandfather's early life. It is in no way exceptional. It is the typical history of a socialist agitator, a working-class leader, in these stark pioneer years.

You will find many present-day Labour town councillors, county councillors, Members of Parliament, trade union officials, who can tell a very similar story.

One of my last memories of my grandfather is also my saddest.

The Fife Miners' Union is situated at the bottom of Rose Street, Dunfermline. My grandfather's home was within five minutes' walking distance of his office. Even after he retired he was in the habit of making a daily journey back to the office just to hear and to see how things were going and occasionally lend a hand. This particular day I dropped in to have tea with him. I wondered what could be the matter. He hardly looked up as I came in. Just sat looking into the fire. That was very unlike his usual warm welcome. An aunt was washing-up at the kitchen sink. There was a vehemence and a clatter in the way she lifted and laid each dish that conveyed she too was in no sunny temper. I sat down by the fire, conscious of atmospherics, but not asking any direct question for that is not the way in our family. Grandfather got up and said he thought he would go out for an evening stroll. Immediately he left, my aunt, taut with indignation, told me what had happened. It was too sore a thing for him to have been able to talk about it himself.

He had gone down to the office as usual. He had been standing on the front step looking about him, ready to walk home again. A communist delegate from one of the districts arrived for a miners' meeting. The young man going in met the old man coming out and bawled at him: "What are *you* doing here? I thought we had got rid of all you old buggers!"

One miner can say that to another and by his tone make the words positively an endearment. But there was no kindness, no wisdom, no understanding in the young man's spirit. He might just as well have lifted his fist and struck the old man physically. He could not have hurt more. My grandfather did not go again to the office. His union, his life, all the pride and the labour and hopes he had put into it! Then to end up sitting looking into the fire, sad, perplexed, afraid to go near his old workplace lest he should be spat on. I walked down Rose Street, Dunfermline, the evening I heard of that encounter, with murder in my heart. I think if I had met a known communist I would have been gaoled for manslaughter. That sort of incident told in bald outline may sound silly and trivial. Multiplied a thousand times and repeated all over Great Britain in a thousand different variations, it goes far to explain the dislike and distrust of the

Communist Party that baulks all their efforts to achieve friendly relations with the rest of the working-class movement.

In visiting my old friends in Lochgelly and going through the years with them, I was not engaged in pointless reminiscing. It is all too easy to escape into the past. That is not my purpose. It is the present that concerns me.

I have said that I would try to journey to the heart of my present discontents. I have not forgotten that, although I may seem to be going about it in a very roundabout way. But it is only against that Lochgelly background, its history and its present needs, that I can find courage enough to go on. For I am clumsily trying to say a number of things that are not easy to say. That can be pounced on and travestied and made to appear mere insensitive malice.

For several years now I have lived with a great fear; the fear that my grandfather's movement is a doomed thing. The fear that it is destined to travel the same road as the pre-Hitler socialist movement of Germany. And for the same discreditable reasons. Not because it has championed the cause of the poor too strenuously, but because, again and again, since 1926, when it ought to have stood its ground, it has found plausible reasons for running away.

And added to all that, making the situation just so much more impossible, because of the failure of a vast hinterland of comfortably situated people in this country who hate fascism as much as I do, to realize that they can only preserve their liberties by making common cause with working-people who perforce must primarily fight for bread.

Those are precisely the mistakes that the organized working-class movement of Germany and liberal-minded, middle-class Germans made in the years before Hitler came to power.

The German social-democrats thought they could conquer by everlastingly retreating. Well-to-do German liberals thought they could enjoy their privileges without paying for them. Civil liberty, intellectual and spiritual liberty were very precious to them. But so was their property. They left too many German workers to face the threat of fascism on empty stomachs. A democracy that had reduced them to bare bone poverty and kept giving them reasons why they should agree to become still poorer, did not seem to vast numbers of German workers such a dazzling thing to fight for.

It says much for the political consciousness of the poverty-tormented German working-class that even in those circumstances, Hitler failed to secure a majority in the last free (*sic*) election held under the Weimar Republic.

It is no answer for well-to-do liberals to reply that fascism aggravates every one of the economic grievances of the poor and takes away even their right to grumble. I know that. All organized working-class movements know that. But in Britain, as in Germany, there are millions of submerged families who do not. So long as "fighting for democracy" suggests to them merely fighting for the continuance of the *status quo*, they are not going to be greatly excited about it. It is asking a great deal of an unemployed or underpaid working-man that he should not be inclined to believe that a change of any kind must be for the better. It is on that sort of mood that fascism, not at all necessarily under that name, knows how to batten.

Has my grandfather's movement no chance at all? I have built my whole life around it. Its history and hopes are mine, too. I cannot remember a time when I was not avidly concerned for its welfare. It is utterly impossible for me to think of myself as other than part of it. But that has not saved me in the last few years from periods of utter despair.

I know the correct doctrinal rebuke to that sort of admission. I have used it myself too often not to know it. And when I say I have despaired I am not thinking of one hundred years from now or even of what may or may not occur in five or ten years' time. I am thinking of the plain, inescapable fact that in the last few years while the ruling class of England has been fighting the class war both at home and abroad with magnificent abandon, as many graves in Spain can testify, the British Labour Movement has been timorously on the retreat.

I have been driven to write this book by the conflict of two very strong emotions. A great fear and a still greater hope. There have been times when it has been fear that has had the ascendancy. I have not tried to hide that. I don't see any point in doing so. Fake optimism convinces no one. You may be able to dodge along on it for a little time but in the long run it is more debilitating than the blackest pessimism.

But if war does not come before the end of the year—which is a very big IF indeed[1]—an important new factor which is beginning to influence public opinion in this country may have time to make itself felt. A new factor that, unless the Labour movement is too conservative to know what to do with it, might be used to revolutionize both the domestic and foreign policy of Great Britain.

For here is what I find happening all over the country. Millions of people, some rich, some poor, mostly neither very much the one nor the other, who before 1932 regarded politics as no affair of theirs, as an unmitigated bore, are radically changing.

All that has happened in Europe in the last seven years is at last beginning to have its effect. The strident voice of Herr Hitler is steadily battering down complacency, the easy-going neutrality of those who thought they could live pleasantly aloof from the vulgar noises and odours of public affairs. The shock and the horror of watching German fascism impose all the tortures of the damned on millions of innocent people, has been strong medicine, criminally, tragically strong, but at least it has stung the world into a new wakefulness and awareness.

In Great Britain to-day, in addition to the traditional

[1] War HAS come, but that does not destroy this hope. Indeed it makes its fulfilment all the more urgent.

followers of the Labour movement, there is an all-important hinterland of concerned people who for the first time in their lives are having their peace of mind invaded by political issues. They are liberty-loving, kind-spirited people. They abhor everything that fascism stands for. They are numerous and influential enough to turn the political balance in favour of whatever party in the state can command their confidence and respect.

I know that to be true. I have talked with them all over Great Britain. I have worked with many of them in all kinds of anti-fascist activities. A considerable number of them are professional workers. I think I understand their language almost as well as I understand the language of Lochgelly colliers.

If only these two can learn to understand one another's values! But there is no use pretending that is easy.

When first Hitler came to power in Germany I went through a period of queer, conflicting emotions. One part of me wanted to rush to the aid of all his victims, caring nothing as to what their class, race or religion might be. But another part of me looked on at the stream of middle-class professional people who came scurrying out of Germany and snarled; damn you, poor folks can't run like you. Why should you expect *me* to help you? I met some of you inside Germany in your pleasant homes. You were charming, cultured, cosmopolitan in your interests, but you lived very happily cheek by jowl with millions of fellow Germans unemployed, hungry, hopeless. Despair turned many of your neighbours towards Hitler. You are being punished now. The dear delights of intellectual liberty that mean so much to you have been broken over your heads. You have had to uproot yourselves from your lovely houses and gardens. Some of you have contrived to get your wealth, or part of it, out ahead of you. Others of you are now as nakedly poor as the German unemployed worker whose shadow darkened your door through all your comfortable years if only you had had eyes to see him, heart to pity him, *camaraderie* enough to make common cause with him even although it had cost you some of your material privileges.

I went to Berlin in the summer of 1933. Wondering if it was entirely a discreet thing to do, I sent a note to a German lady of great wealth and vivacity whom I had known in the pre-Hitler period. We met first in 1929 at an international peace conference in London. I promised that next time I came to Germany I would call on her. "Next" time was September 1930, on a homeward journey from Russia. I telephoned from a Berlin hotel and inside an hour an exotic outsize bouquet of roses was spilling all over my minute back bedroom and an elegant car was waiting outside to take me along to a party that was going on at my friend's house.

It was then I met her husband. We wrangled good-temperedly about some current political affairs. He was a liberal. I was a socialist. With a friendly, mischievous smile, he made a point of showing me a signed

253

photograph of Hindenburg that occupied the place of honour on his desk. He was every inch a patriot, very proud of being German. No one could have seemed more on top of the world than my charming host as I remember him then, with distinguished artists and scholars, as well as merely fashionable people surrounding him in his very grand home. That was the only time I met him. Before I returned to Berlin Hitler had come to power. My friend's husband had been driven to commit suicide. In 1933 she was alone when I called. The vast drawing-room (I think I should say *salon*) that formerly I had seen crowded with gay chattering people, was now a ghostly room to walk through. There were exquisite paintings by Cézanne and Gauguin on the walls. But the master of the house was dead. He had been too unhappy to want to go on living. Great possessions may be very important, but they look very paltry in the home of a man who has committed suicide.

Millions of Germans learned too late that wealth cannot buy laughter, nor lighthearted fooling, nor peace of mind, nor even any real comfort once the spiritual values of a household are slain.

To people in Britain very like some of my German friends who loved liberty but were not wise enough to see in time what they must do to preserve it, let me, without taking time to look round for tactful words in which to do it, blurt out what has often been in my mind in those last seven years.

From the first day you started to campaign and

collect for German refugees I ran by your side, campaigned and collected with you. This was my concern as well as yours. I kicked back into the hinterland of my emotions another me that kept scowling and muttering, what about *my* folks, what about underpaid colliers, what about Lanarkshire slums, what about youngsters leaving school with no jobs to go to, what about indigent (that's the sort of word you use, isn't it?) old people, and working-class mothers driven from pillar to post with the daily, hourly struggle to keep the pot boiling, and shoes mended and finding an extra shilling so that Mary and John can go to the "Pictures" or to the dance that the rest of their pals are going to?

It was not that I was less concerned than you about the suffering of Hitler's victims. But I was continually irritated with what seemed to me the lopsided nature of your sympathies. Nothing was too much trouble if it was on behalf of German refugees. But you had sometimes difficulty in disguising your impatience when asked to give your serious attention to sufferers nearer home.

I had moods when my thoughts about you were anything but kind, when I asked what was wrong with your eyes, your mind, your imagination? Was your palate so jaded that you had to have suffering presented to you in sensational, sadistic form before it got through to your senses? The blood streaming, the victim screaming, a Nazi gaoler standing in the background with a rubber truncheon in his raised hand, a good hot juicy atrocity story written in underneath in heavy black type.

Apparently it meant nothing to you to go through Blantyre or Merthyr or Glasgow slums where all that the naked eye can see is a greyness. Not the bright red of streaming blood and the deep blue-black of the marks left by a whip. Just greyness. Just unspectacular, unspiced grey. People going on living without much hope, strangled by poverty, grey faces, grey clothes, shabby grey streets. There are plenty of bruises in such places. But they don't show in the sort of ways that titivate the senses. Take an eager young Welshman, leave him for five or ten years without work, not wanted, no money, too downed to feel like reading or doing anything at all with the long empty hours, and you produce bruises all right.

I can hear protests and denials. "We dislike suffering and injustice wherever we find it. We always help as much as we can. There has never been a Lord Mayor's fund that we did not subscribe to." Yes, yes, I know. To the poor inside your own country you give cash. But to the victims of German fascism you give more than cash. Your sympathy is of an essentially different kind. You give your peace of mind. You are invaded, overwhelmed, made unhappy.

For you have identified yourself with those whom Hitler persecutes. That is as it should be. But for me the victims of poverty and of fascism are one and the same. Liberty and preventable poverty cannot live together. Intellectual freedom and racial tolerance

are not secure and do not earn the right to be secure
in any society in which large numbers of people are
tormented by social wrongs.

I do not say those things in order to wound. I say
them because I am feverishly anxious to see new alignments in the political life of Great Britain. New alignments arising from a solid, honest recognition that the
fight against the maltreatment of human beings begins
at home. On that basis we could do great things in this
country. On any other basis I see nothing for it except
that we muddle and dawdle along for a little time
longer until calamity overtakes us.

EPILOGUE

THIS book is no more than a personal and political scrap-book telling something of the life and values of a Scottish mining community. It deals mainly with the years following the last war and is halted abruptly by the outbreak of the present one.

I began to write it in the hope of seeing my own way more clearly through the tangle of recent years. Once begun, I found that the earlier chapters practically wrote themselves. I had a very happy, carefully sheltered childhood. Then to add to my good fortune, my most impressionable adolescent years were lived during the most vigorous and alive period in the history of our mining communities. I mean from about 1916 until the post-war slump in trade began to close in around us.

From that time onwards everything became very different. In terms of external circumstances I no doubt seemed to be doing very well. Two years after graduating from Edinburgh University I was thrown into Parliament. Three years later I was thrown out again. When that happened one bit of me was disappointed and annoyed. But another bit threw its hat in the air and shouted joyfully "Now let's see the world!"

After being defeated in the 1931 general election I told myself that my life and my time were my own again. What a delusion that always is! I certainly managed to go hoboing more than half way across the

258

world. I had all the fun of the fair: new places, new people, new experiences.

But all the time there was the steady jag, jag, jag, of a sad undercurrent of emotions.

There was the feeling of impending tragedy in the air. Nothing was working out in the post-war world as we had planned it should. What sort of brave new social order was this that we had purchased by slaughtering ten million men? The world had not even learned the rudiments of good manners. Wherever I went I found the same revolting contrasts. Some people over-wealthy, over-pampered, over-privileged: others with not even enough to eat.

I lived with unemployed German colliers in the Ruhr. I lived with unemployed Scottish colliers in Lanarkshire. I reversed the usual process of fashionable ladies slumming in the poorer quarters of their cities. I went slumming in the West End of London. I went slumming in the West End of Berlin. I found the life of the rich in every country pretty much the same. I found the lot of the poor, whether German or British, almost identical.

Cutting across all national boundaries it seemed to me that the main problem of the times was the fight against poverty.

I am being asked to fight against Germany instead. "No, not against Germany, against Hitler," is the standard reply. And the reply is made in the loudest and brassiest tones by those in high places in British politics who right up to the outbreak of war were

Hitler's most ardent admirers. Over a wide field of thought and action they still are. Their only genuine complaint against him is that he should dare to challenge British supremacy instead of marching into the Soviet Ukraine as they had counted on him to do.

But for the purposes of the war and so long as it lasts, every man Jack of that profoundly anti-democratic section of the British propertied classes will use the language of liberty, equality, fraternity.

Then, if we do not walk warily, if the levers of power remain in those same hands, there will be the same tragic aftermath as last time, the same unfulfilled promises.

In these sober September days, with an atmosphere of waiting and watching everywhere, no one quite sure what the next move is going to be, there are many people in Great Britain who confidently assert that millions of Germans inside Germany hate Hitler as much as we do: that their efforts added to ours will soon overthrow the Nazi regime and open up a way to peace.

I do not believe it is going to be as simple as that. We have given the German people too many bitter memories. If we ourselves had been wiser and kinder the likelihood of a quick riddance of Hitler would have been much greater. But then, if we had been wiser and kinder, a Hitler could never in the first place have achieved power in Germany.

The major tragedy of the last twenty-five years is not how Europe went to war in 1914–18, but how the victorious allies lost the peace in the twenty years that followed.

At this moment the German nation is being lashed into a furious hatred of all things British. It is not what happened on the battlefields between 1914 and '18 that gives Hitler his power. It is the ugly, undeniable, inexcusable story of the six months following the armistice, when, though victorious on the field of battle, the allied powers refused to allow food to reach German women and children whom they knew to be starving.

Against that charge a flat denial is no use. It does not convince a single man or woman, least of all a single German, for the facts are against us. I believe that we can destroy Hitlerism only if we have the courage to face the truth and are not afraid to state it. I don't believe we can win allies among the German masses by meeting lies with lies, evasions with evasions. Nor need we fear the truth as much as all that. For though the statesmen who met at Versailles disgraced us, a quarter of a million British soldiers quartered in the Rhineland redeemed our good name. Do you know this? Have you forgotten it? If so now is the time to recall it for it is the most cleansing memory left by the last war.

The armistice had been signed but the blockade against Germany was being rigidly enforced. A quarter of a million British soldiers were quartered in the Rhineland. Ample rations were sent in to them so that they need not be affected by the blockade. But for all that, Lord Plumer who commanded the British Army of Occupation in Germany had to send frenzied telegrams to London and Geneva reporting that the physical efficiency of his men was being undermined by malnutrition. Our soldiers had, as I have said, ample food rations. But no power on earth could prevent the ordinary decent fellows who made up the British Army of Occupation from sharing those rations with the starving German population they were living among.

That memory is very precious to me. I hold on tightly to it. It is the basis of all my hopes. It is an integral part of the story this book tries to tell. If only Europe in those last twenty years had been governed in the spirit of those rank and file soldiers! For left to their own natural impulses, people are kind to one another. I mean ordinary working people. The mischief begins when Brass Hats and power-drunk politicians, the spokesmen of rich privileged minorities in any community are allowed to dictate policy. For they forget about humble people and their needs. Property is everything. People of very little account.

In the British army that occupied the Rhineland at the end of the last war there was a good sprinkling of Fifeshire colliers.

When demobilization at last came and our men returned to Fife they were in a revolutionary mood. They expected a new vastly improved world. I was fourteen years old then and shared their expectations. We wanted ordinary working people in all countries, victors and vanquished alike, to be given the chance of a good life. We wanted hates and punishments to end with the war. There were many who thought like that in the colliery districts.

But in the twenty-one years that have followed, our hopes and the policies we advocated have been as completely routed as the Kaiser's armies.

The later chapters of this book were not easy for me to write. For I have been bound to consider how far our defeats have been our own fault. The Labour Movement that I have known in my twenties and early thirties has entirely failed to scale up to the size of events. It has hesitated when it ought to have been certain of itself. It has retreated when it ought to have advanced. It has been too dangerously timid, too depressingly orthodox, too unsure of its distinctive purposes to inspire general confidence.

Political parties and politicians have not left me much that I feel I dare rely on. But there is one unfailing source of sustenance that no one can take away. That is my sure knowledge of the sanity and kindness of ordinary working people whom I have known and loved in this country and in Germany too. I believe that the world can be redeemed only by such as they.

I believe that so far as Great Britain is different from Germany, so far as Great Britain is better than Germany, it is so to the extent that such people are not so utterly powerless here as there. But the ordinary unpretentious kind-spirited people everywhere are always much too modest. They lack the arrogance of their mission.

Between the last war and this one I have watched British as well as German workers patiently endure a shabby, cruel, makeshift kind of world. I cannot believe that they will once more wade through Hell and not at long last learn that they must take the control of affairs into their own hands.

Internationalism in politics has broken down. But the internationality of common experience still remains. I believe that gentleness and common sense can emerge in world affairs only when Fifeshire colliers and Lanarkshire colliers and all such as they can get together with their opposite numbers inside Germany. For ordinary people everywhere speak the same language. They understand one another when they meet. That was how it was twenty years ago on the Rhineland. But they have not had much say in affairs since then. It is the exceptional people who have been running the world. It is the exceptional people, rich, privileged, supposedly cultured who got us into the last war, who made the Peace Treaties, who have governed us since, who got us into this war. To say that Hitler and Hitler alone is responsible for all that is happening now, is the language of social and political illiteracy, Hitler is a mad evil thing that must be got rid of. But so must the social soil that breeds such creatures. That is a much bigger job. That is what we failed to do last time. But to-morrow we will have other opportunities. To-morrow is a new day.

264